Software Defined Storage

with OpenStack Swift

by Joe Arnold

Published by SwiftStack, Inc.,
340 Brannan Street, Suite 501, San Francisco, CA 94107

Printed in the United Stated of America.

ISBN: 978-0-9892421-0-3

First published: April 2013. First Edition.

Software Defined Storage

with OpenStack Swift

Table of Contents

Chapter 2, cont.

Preface

What is Software Defined Storage?

The catalyst for starting SwiftStack in 2011 was the pain I experienced first-hand from deploying, managing and using vendor-specific storage systems. As a user, what I wanted was more flexibility, less lock-in, better control, and lower costs than what traditional storage systems could provide. I also heard the same thing from other organizations - and with data growing dramatically (but not IT budgets), there was absolute certainty that these difficulties would persist and grow, not just for me, but for pretty much everyone who stored and served data at scale.

When SwiftStack was started, our big idea was to provide an object storage system – OpenStack Swift – with a de-coupled management system so customers could achieve (1) amazing flexibility in terms of how (and where) they deployed their storage, (2) control of their data without being locked-in to a vendor and (3) private storage at public cloud prices.

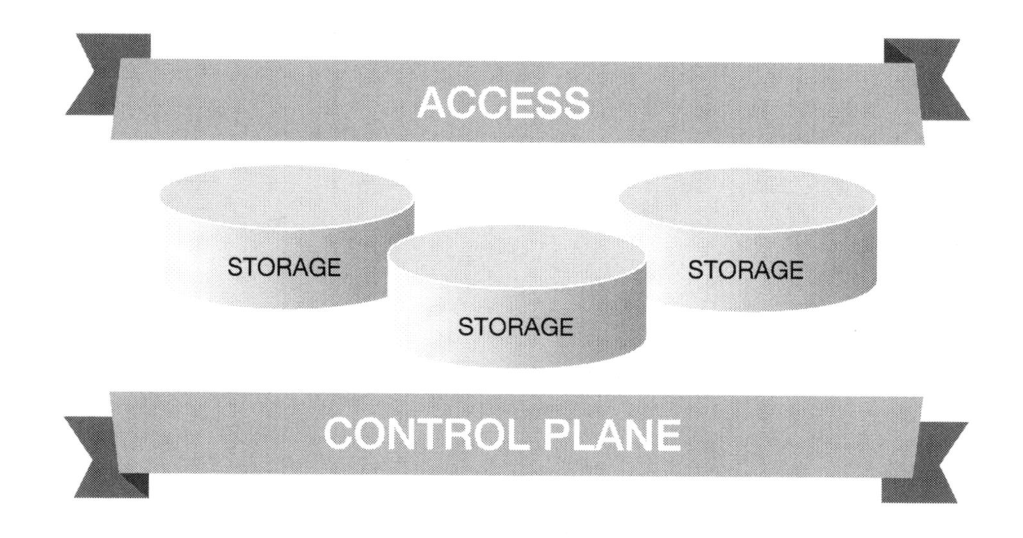

These features are the essence of Software Defined Storage (SDS), a new term the meaning of which is still being defined. We think the term perfectly illustrates the fundamental change that Swift represents. Key aspects of SDS are scalability, adaptability, and the ability to use most any hardware. Through this de-coupling, operators can now make choices on how their storage is scaled and managed and how users can store and access data – all driven programmatically for the entire storage tier, regardless of where the storage resources are deployed.

Why OpenStack Swift?

In the summer of 2010, one of the two core projects during the launch of OpenStack was an object storage system called Swift. Because Swift was already running in production at Rackspace, this release allowed organizations to deploy storage infrastructure that is not just API compatible with public cloud storage, but architecturally identical.

The industry had seen how powerful an HTTP-based object storage system could be and I was fortunate to have had a front row seat as part of the team building one of the first widely-used platform-as-a-service running on top of Amazon Web Services. Amazon popularized HTTP-addressable object storage with their wildly successful Simple Storage Service (S3).

Swift allows for a wide spectrum of uses, from supporting web/mobile applications, backup, and active archive. With the layering of additional services, users can access the storage via its native HTTP API, or use command-line tools, file system gateways (for CIFS/NFS), or easy-to-use applications to store and sync data with their desktops, tablets, and mobile devices.

But what was really interesting is what happens 'under the hood'. Swift was a fundamentally new storage system. It wasn't a single, *monolithic* system, but rather a *distributed* system. Not only that, Swift is a change in how storage works. It isn't an attempt to be like other storage systems and mimic their interfaces. Swift was an eventually-consistent storage system. This comes with some constraints, to be sure, but it is a perfect match for web, mobile, and as-a-service applications.

Because of these benefits I co-founded a company dedicated to improving and providing Swift solutions at SwiftStack. SwiftStack has been able to bring some of the founders of Swift onboard, as well as other developers contributing to Swift.

At SwiftStack, we have learned much from real-world deployments – large and small which we will share with you throughout this book. Now, Swift is becoming more and more widespread and is evolving into a standard way to store and distribute large amounts of data.

This book aims to help newcomers learn from our experiences. Our goal is to get you up and running more quickly and easily, making your successful conversion to Swift, well ... swifter.

Who Should Read this Book?

Software Defined Storage with OpenStack Swift is written for deployers, operators, and developers interested in using Swift. While it's not necessary to read this book cover-to-cover, we make an attempt to cover the topics in logical order.

That being said, here are a few short-cuts:

- If you're responsible for designing and architecting a Swift cluster, check out Chapter 6.
- If you're a developer, head straight to Chapter 3 to learn about the Swift API.
- If you are a systems admin wanting to get up and running check out Chapters 4 and 7.
- If you want to get a good high-level overview of Swift keep reading through Chapter 2.
- While the book assumes a familiarity with basic Linux administration, networking, and storage. It also attempts to explain Swift in clear and

simple terms so that anyone can understand the basic concepts and principles (see Chapters 1 and 2).

What's in this Book?

The book begins by charting the explosive growth of data and data storage and how this led to the development of Swift (Chapter 1), a durable, scalable, concurrent, and open source object storage system. From there it examines the conceptual underpinnings of Swift, covering basic terms (including objects, containers, and the ring), its architecture, and how it works (Chapter 2).

Chapter 3 covers the details of how to use Swift and presents some of its most powerful and useful features. This chapter is great for developers to become familiar with the Swift API. It also covers the very handy **swift** command-line tool that can run anywhere Python can. For those building applications, you'll find some examples in popular programming languages, as well as a survey of client tools.

From there, *The not quite complete guide to Software Defined Storage with OpenStack Swift*, dives into specifics, leading you through all the steps in the process of working with, installing, operating, and tuning Swift.

Chapter 4 covers the installation process of Swift and will get you up and running quickly.

Chapter 5 explains the features and capabilities of the SwiftStack Controller.

Chapter 6 details the hardware required to run a Swift cluster and digs deeper into network configs and hardware requirements for Swift.

Next, in Chapter 7 you'll learn about the operational aspects of Swift. It's not a matter of if hardware fails, it's when! So in this chapter you'll find out what to do about it.

Chapter 8 will briefly touch on integrations with Swift. Mostly it covers authentication and, in less detail, the possibilities for integrating with content-delivery networks. You can also read about some of the integrations that our customers have found useful.

Chapter 9 details testing and benchmarking best practices for varied Swift deployments.

In chapter Chapter 10, you'll figure out how to get your Swift cluster tuned up. This includes benchmarking and the myriad tuning parameters available in Swift. Familiarity with these is critical for getting the most out of your cluster.

Conventions Used in this Book

The following typographical conventions are used in this book:

Italic
Indicates new terms, special emphasis, URLs, email addresses, filenames, and extensions.

`Constant width`
Used for program listings, as well as within paragraphs to refer to program elements such as variable or function names, databases, data types, environment variables, statements, and keywords.

`Constant width bold`
Shows commands or other text that should be typed literally by the user.

`Constant width italic`
Shows text that should be replaced with user-supplied values or values determined by context.

Using Code Examples

This book aims to help you work effectively with Swift. In general, you may use the code in this book in your programs and documentation. You do not need to contact us for permission unless you're reproducing a significant portion of the code. For example, writing a program that uses several chunks of code from this book does not require permission. Selling or distributing a CD-ROM of examples does require permission. Answering a question by citing this book and quoting example code does not require permission. Incorporating a significant amount of example code from this book into your product's documentation does require permission.

We appreciate, but do not require, attribution. An attribution usually includes the title, author, and publication year. For example: "*Software Defined Storage with OpenStack Swift*, First Edition, by Joe Arnold. Copyright 2013."

If you feel your use of code examples falls outside fair use or the permission given here, feel free to contact us via email (*contact@swiftstack.com*).

How to Contact Us

SwiftStack provides a software-defined storage system for OpenStack Swift. Our solution combines a unique, decoupled storage Controller with OpenStack Swift that provides our customers with cost-effective, scale-out storage running on commodity hardware.

The company was founded in 2011 to help operations teams implement and manage an easy-to-use, multi-tenant, and highly scalable cloud storage platform. Our product is compatible with Ubuntu, RedHat Enteprise Linux, and CentOS and can run on a wide-range of hardware.

SwiftStack is headquartered in San Francisco, California with support operations covering Asian and European timezones. To contact us, you can email *contact@swiftstack.com*. If you have specific questions for me, you can email me at *joe@swiftstack.com*.

We'd Like to Hear From You

As you use this book and work with Swift and SwiftStack, we invite your comments and feedback. From the very start, Swift has benefited from the contributions of hundreds of developers and users. And we hope that doesn't stop.

This book was written quite quickly. We wanted to be able to put it in your hands at the OpenStack Summit (April 15-18, 2013) and we're proud of what we've put together. But we also want to produce a second edition and we invite your comments, feedback, and suggestions. Please let us know what we need to correct or add; share your insights; and help us create a resource that will serve you better. You can do so by visiting *http://swiftstack.com/book/*.

Acknowledgements

There are over a hundred developers who have contributed to Swift. I'd like to thank each one of them for their ongoing contributions. There are also hundreds of operators of Swift who count on a stable, reliable storage system. Without them, Swift would just be an interesting idea. So, I would like to thank all of the Swift operators for trusting us with your data.

This book couldn't have come together without the support of a large cast. Everyone at SwiftStack has contributed to writing this book. I'd like to especially thank a few people: Anders Tjernlund for thinking we should write this book in the first place, writing so much, and driving the whole process; John Dickinson for providing his insight into the formation of Swift; Darrell Bishop for lending his deep operational expertise with large-scale private clusters; Clay McClure for diving deep into how to use Swift; Martin Lanner for sharing his experience building, managing, and benchmarking Swift clusters; Hugo Kuo for his expert hand configuring Swift; Melinda Graham who provided critical feedback; Jan Meyer who designed and produced the book and accompanying graphics; and to Mark Feldman without whom this book project would not have come together.

CHAPTER ONE

Meet Swift

Swift was a thoughtful and creative response to the unprecedented and precipitous growth in data, much of which needs to be stored forever. In 2009 a group of developers and engineers including Will Reese, Greg Holt, John Dickinson, Jay Payne, Michael Barton, Greg Lange, and Chuck Thier - all then with Rackspace - started developing what would become Swift. Working collaboratively for about a year, in a small, cramped office in San Antonio, TX, they came up with an object storage system that was a drop-in replacement for an existing storage system designed to compete with Amazon S3. The goals of this project were to build a simple system with could scale; durably store petabytes upon petabytes of data; and be extremely available. What came out of this work was Swift.

In 2010 the OpenStack project began and Swift (along with Nova) was one of its first two projects. With the launch of Swift, the world had an open-source storage system that had been proven to run at extremely large scale.

Swift is an object storage system that differs from traditional storage systems which are either block or file. Instead, Swift uses principles of eventual consistency. This means that Swift is capable of scaling to an extremely large number of concurrent connections and extremely large sets of data. Since its launch in 2011, Swift has added hundreds of contributors, gotten even more stable, become faster, and added many great, new features.

In this chapter you'll learn about the boom in unstructured data and its particular storage requirements; how this led to the development of OpenStack Swift; Swift's basic features and many benefits for developers and IT operators; and how Swift's object storage system compares to more familiar block and file storage.

The Growth of Data

Exabytes of Data

In this era of connected devices, the demands on storage systems are increasing exponentially. Users are producing and consuming more data than ever. Social media, online video, user-uploaded content, gaming, and software-as-a-service applications are all contributing to the vast need for easily accessible storage systems that can grow without bounds. To understand the scale of this growth in data, consider that in 2012 the International Data Corporation (IDC) declared that the volume of digital content worldwide exceeded 2,765 exabytes. This was an increase of almost 2,048 exabytes in 2 short years.

So, how much is an exabyte of data? It's an almost unimaginably large quantity, but let's try. It's equivalent to about 1 thousand petabytes, 1 million terabytes, or 1 billion gigabytes. These figures will be meaningful to some, but if they're not, we'll contextualize this a bit more. Books are on the order of about 1 MB. The largest library in the world, the Library of Congress has about 23 millions volumes, which would total only approximate 23TB of data. High resolution photos are on the order of 2 MB; an exabyte would be 536,870,900 high resolution photos.

And stored data is continuing to grow at ever faster rates. By 2020, the IDC estimates that the amount of data in the world will reach 3,5840 exabytes. Divided by the world's population, that is 4 TB per person.

Examples of Unstructured Data

What is all this data? The majority of it is 'unstructured' data. This means that the data does not have a pre-defined data model and is typically stored as a file as opposed to an entry in a database (which would be structured data.) Much of this unstructured data is the ever proliferating photos, videos, emails, documents, instant messages, and texts – all generated on billions of devices, with more coming on-line each year. Users are producing and consuming more data than ever. By the end of 2012, Facebook users were uploading 350 million new photos each day. That's 7 petabytes per month; enough to keep the folks at Facebook continuously building data centers.

Requirements for Storing Unstructured Data

Storage of unstructured data needs to ensure durability, accessibility, low cost, and manageability.

Durability: Even though you might never look at your old vacation photos again, Flickr needs to store them forever. In fact, most unstructured data needs to be kept forever in order to meet customer expectations and or legal and regulatory requirements.

Accessibility: Unstructured data also needs to be available in an instant, via a variety of devices - primarily mobile phones and web browsers. While some data can be archived, users expect most of their data to be immediately available.

Low Cost: Unstructured data needs to be stored at low cost. With enough money, any storage problem can be solved. However, we live in a world of constraints. Business models and available budgets necessitate low cost data storage solutions.

Manageability: With larger storage systems coming online, manageability becomes critical. Software-defined storage in the data center enables ease of management. We routinely have a small number of administrators support a large number of storage servers. This is only possible with a decoupled controller to manage the storage system.

No One-size-fits-all Storage System

While it would be great if there was a one-size-fits-all solution, there isn't. Storage systems entail tradeoffs that we can think of as responses to their particular requirements and circumstances. The CAP-theorem, first advanced by Eric Brewster (UC Berkeley, Computer Science) in 2000 succinctly frames the problem. It states that distributed computer systems cannot simultaneously provide consistency, availability, and partition tolerance. Practically this means that you're left to choose the two that are most important for your particular circumstances.

If the system needs consistency (say you're a bank recording account balances), then either availability or partition tolerance would need to suffer. This is typically what is needed for transactional workloads such as supporting databases. If you want availability and partition tolerance, then you need to tolerate being occasionally inconsistent.

The bottom line is that it's impossible to build a system that can address all three: consistency, availability, and partition tolerance. Purpose-built storage systems will offer an operator more reliability for a particular workload than a general-purpose storage system designed to support all workloads.

Swift, however, is up to the task of handling the workloads required for large amounts of unstructured data. Following the CAP-theorem, Swift sacrifices consistency to gain availability and partition tolerance. This allows Swift to be very durable and highly available.

The Origins of Swift: From the Small to the Open

recalled fondly by John Dickinson

In 2008, Rackspace developed its Rackspace Cloud Files cloud storage service as a response to customer demands and as an answer to Amazon's Simple Storage Service (S3). The underlying technology developed for the first iteration of Rackspace Cloud Files was great up to a point but frankly required a lot of time, effort, and money to scale. With unstructured data growing so rapidly, we knew we needed something better. So in August 2009, Rackspace set a team to work developing a complete, ground up replacement for their initial cloud storage platform. I was fortunate to be on the original project team, code-named "Swift."

A team of about nine of us set to work. None of us had specific roles. Mostly we sat around in a small, often hot room on the fourth floor in downtown San Antonio, identifying the hard problems we needed to solve. We were trying to figure out how we would deploy Swift, what the network would look like, what the infrastructure to support it was going to look like - all that good stuff. We were very collaborative, but also we would compete to arrive at the best solution. We'd think about a problem and then go home. Two people would come back the next day with implementations for it and we'd choose the one we thought was best. There was a really great team dynamic and it was an awesome experience. Ideas were always flying around that room and some of them were crazy. But some of them worked out really well.

We worked on this for about a year and in July 2010, as part of the OpenStack project which Rackspace co-founded with NASA, we released the source code for Swift under the Apache 2 license. We contributed the Cloud Files Swift Code which became OpenStack Object Storage. In October 2010, a subsequent release of Swift, named "Austin," which included the compute orchestration framework contributed by NASA, was made public. The first commercial deployments of Swift outside Rackspace were at Korea Telecom and Internap, which used Swift to provide public cloud storage services. (That's how I came to know Joe Arnold and ultimately join SwiftStack.) Swift is now used by web companies, business of all sizes, life sciences companies, research organizations, and service providers worldwide.

In the end, I think we created the kernel of a great cloud storage platform and I am proud to have been part of that. But it is also very gratifying to be part of something larger. When Rackspace Hosting made a short video about how Swift was made, we chose to end with a shot of text receding into star-filled outer space. Our invocation of *Star Wars* was partly tongue in cheek, and partly serious. We really did and still do feel that we're part of a growing rebel force fighting the emergence of proprietary cloud stacks and creating a standard way to deploy applications and connect clouds. We're still part of the minority, but our forces and capacities are growing, in large part because more and more companies and developers are working with OpenStack.

OpenStack Swift

Swift is a multi-tenant, highly scalable, and durable object storage system designed to store large amounts of unstructured data at low cost. Highly scalable means that it can scale from a few nodes and a handful of drives to thousands of machines with multiple petabytes of storage. Swift is designed to be horizontally scalable so there is no single point-of-failure.

Swift is used by businesses of all sizes, service providers, and research organizations worldwide. It is typically used to store unstructured data such as documents, web content, backups, images, and virtual machine snapshots. Originally developed as the engine behind RackSpace Cloud Files in 2010, it was open-sourced under the Apache 2 license as part of the OpenStack project. With more than 100 companies and thousands of developers now participating in the OpenStack project, the usage of Swift is increasing rapidly.

Swift is not a traditional file system or a raw block device (for more about other object storage systems see below). Instead, it enables you to store, retrieve, and delete objects (with their associated metadata) in containers ("buckets" in Amazon S3 terminology) via a RESTful HTTP API. Developers can either write directly to the Swift API or use one of the many client libraries that exist for all popular programming languages, such as Java, Python, Ruby, and C#.

Below we cover some of the key characteristics and capacities of Swift.

Scalable

Swift is designed to scale linearly based on how much data needs to be stored and how many users need to be served. This means that it can scale from a few nodes and a handful of drives to thousands of machines with dozens, even hundreds of petabytes of storage. As the system grows in usage and the number of requests increase, performance doesn't degrade. To scale up, the system grows where needed — by adding storage nodes to increase storage capacity, adding proxy nodes as requests increase, and growing network capacity where bottlenecks are detected.

Durable

With its innovative, distributed architecture, Swift is extremely durable. To achieve this level of durability, objects are distributed in triplicate across the cluster. A write must be confirmed in two of the three locations to be considered successful. Auditing processes run to ensure that good data doesn't go bad. Replicators run to ensure that a sufficient number of copies are in the cluster. In the event that a device fails, data is replicated throughout the cluster to ensure that three good copies remain.

Swift is also durable because of its ability to define failure zones. Failure zones allow a cluster to be deployed across physical boundaries, each of which could individually fail. For example, a cluster could be deployed across several nearby data centers, enabling it to survive multiple datacenter failures.

Swift also enables a cluster to span multiple regions and multiple, high-latency data centers. This enables data to be accessed from each region, or for one region to be a disaster-recovery site.

Highly Concurrent

Available storage space isn't a useful statistic on its own. More useful and important is the storage system's concurrency. The ability to handle a great number of simultaneous connections from within a datacenter or across the web is critical to satisfy the needs of applications that are built for web scale usage.

Swift uses a shared-nothing approach and employs the same proven techniques that have been used to provide high availability by many web applications.

Open Source

Originally developed in 2010 as the engine behind RackSpace Cloud Files, it was open-sourced under the Apache 2 license as part of the OpenStack project. With more than 100 participating developers as of early 2013, the Swift community is growing every quarter. What makes Swift different from most other open source projects, however, is that Swift had already been tested in large-scale production usage before it was released as part of the OpenStack project. Because Swift is open source there is no vendor lock-in for users. Also the publicly available source code can be reviewed by many more developers than is the case for proprietary software. This means that potential bugs tend to be more visible and more rapidly corrected than is the case with proprietary software. In the long term, "open" generally wins.

Large Ecosystem

With the large number of organizations and developers participating in the OpenStack project or ecosystem, the development velocity, and breadth of tools, utilities and services for Swift is large and will only increase over time. There are many tools, libraries, clients and applications that already support Swift's API. By engaging with this community and ecosystem of tools, you can access and share tools, best practices and deployment know-how with other organizations and community members who are using Swift. This ecosystem is enabled and empowered by Swift's open source code.

Runs on Commodity Hardware

Because Swift is designed from the ground up to handle failures, reliability on the individual component level is less critical and it can thus be run on commodity hardware. Regular desktop drives can be used in a Swift cluster rather than more expensive "enterprise" drives. Hardware quality and configuration can be chosen to suit the tolerances of the application and the ability to replace failed equipment.

Since commodity hardware can be used with the system, there is no lock-in with any particular storage vendor. This means deployments can continually take advantage of decreasing hardware prices and increasing drive capacity.

Developer Friendly

Swift offers many benefits for developers. You can serve data directly over the internet. Swift can be a single storage system for application assets - a simple and elegant solution for all involved. Having a single storage system can free you up to focus on app development. Lastly, you can benefit from the rich and growing ecosystem of Swift tools and libraries.

Beyond the Swift's core functionality to store and serve data durably at large scale, Swift has many built-in features that makes it easy for application developers and end-users to use.

Some of these features include:

> **Static website hosting:** Users can host static websites, including javascript and css, directly from Swift. Swift also supports custom error pages and auto-generate listings.

Automatically expiring objects: Objects can be given an expiry time after which they are no longer available and will be deleted. This is very useful for preventing stale data from remaining available and to comply with data retention policies.

Time-limited URLs: URLs can be generated that are valid for only a limited period of time. These URLs can prevent hotlinking or enable temporary write permissions without needing to hand out full credentials to an untrusted party.

Quotas: Storage limits can be set on containers and accounts.

Direct-from-HTML-form uploads: Users can generate web forms that upload data directly into Swift so that it doesn't have to be proxied through another server

Versioned writes: Users can write a new version of an object and keep all older versions of the object.

Support for chunked Transfer-Encoding: Users can upload data to Swift without knowing ahead of time how large the object is.

Multi-Range reads: Users can read one or more sections of an object with only one read request

Access control lists: Users can configure access to their data to enable or prevent others ability to read or write the data.

Programmatic access to data locality: Deployers can integrate Swift with systems like Hadoop and take advantage of locality information to lower network requirements when processing data.

Operator Friendly

Swift is appealing to IT operators for a number of overlapping reasons. Swift lets you use low-cost, industry-standard servers and disks. With Swift you can manage more data and use cases with ease. It's easy and quick to enable new applications. Finally, Swift's durable architecture with no single-point of failure lets you avoid catastrophic failure and rest a bit easier. The chapters in this book on deploying and operating Swift clusters will provide you with an overview of how easy it really is.

Comparison with Other Storage Systems

Different types of data have different access patterns and therefore can be best stored on different types of storage systems. There are three broad categories of data storage: block storage, file storage, and object storage.

Block storage is storage that has access to raw, unformatted hardware. This kind of storage is useful when speed and space efficiency are most important. The most common use for block storage is databases, which can use a raw block device to efficiently read and write structured data. Databases are ideal for storing relational, customer information.

File storage is what we're most used to seeing on a day-to-day basis. File storage takes a formatted hard drive, like the one on your computer, and exposes a file system on it. You see the file system when you open and close documents on your computer. Although file storage provides a useful abstraction on top of a storage device, it doesn't work very well when you have large amounts of data or when you have high demand for a particular piece of data.

Object storage is probably the least familiar type of storage. Object storage doesn't provide access to raw blocks of data; it doesn't offer file-based access. Object storage provides access to whole objects or blobs of data - and it generally does so with an API specific to that system. Object storage excels at storing content that can grow without bounds. Perfect uses include backups, archiving, and static web content like images and scripts. One of the main advantages of object storage systems is their ability to reliable store a large amount of data at a relatively low cost. Swift is an object storage system. It is not a distributed file system. Swift excels at storing web content and backups and handling massive concurrency.

Conclusion

Now that you've learned about the proliferation in unstructured data that led to the creation of Swift and about some of its most pertinent features, you're ready to learn more about how Swift works (Chapter 2) - at a broad and conceptual level. After that you'll get to dive into the particulars of Swift.

CHAPTER TWO

How Swift Works

In this chapter, we will explain some of the core components and terms, including: the key concepts (accounts, containers, and objects); Swift's architecture; and how Swift works. We'll finish up by walking through a few scenarios to show how all these components work together. This chapter will also introduce you to the basics of the Swift API.

Key Concepts

"Let's start from the very beginning. A very good place to start"
- Maria, from The Sound of Music

A foundational premise of Swift is that requests are made via HTTP using a RESTful API. When a request is made into Swift it is in the form of a URL. A Swift URL has the following components – accounts, containers, and objects. A URL in Swift for an object looks like this:

```
https://swift.example.com/v1/account/container/object
```

Accounts

An account in Swift is a user in the storage system. Unlike other storage systems which create volumes, Swift creates accounts, which enable multiple users and applications to access the storage system at the same time.

Containers

Swift accounts create and store data in individual Containers. containers are namespaces used to group objects within an account. Although containers cannot be nested, they are conceptually similar to directories or folders in a file system.

For convenience, each account in the system has a database that has a record of all of the containers for that account. Likewise, each container database has a record for each object. These databases are not used when directly accessing an object. They are only used when making requests to list objects in a container or containers in an account.

There is no limit to the number of containers that a user may create within a Swift account and the containers do not have globally-unique naming requirements.

Figure 2.1

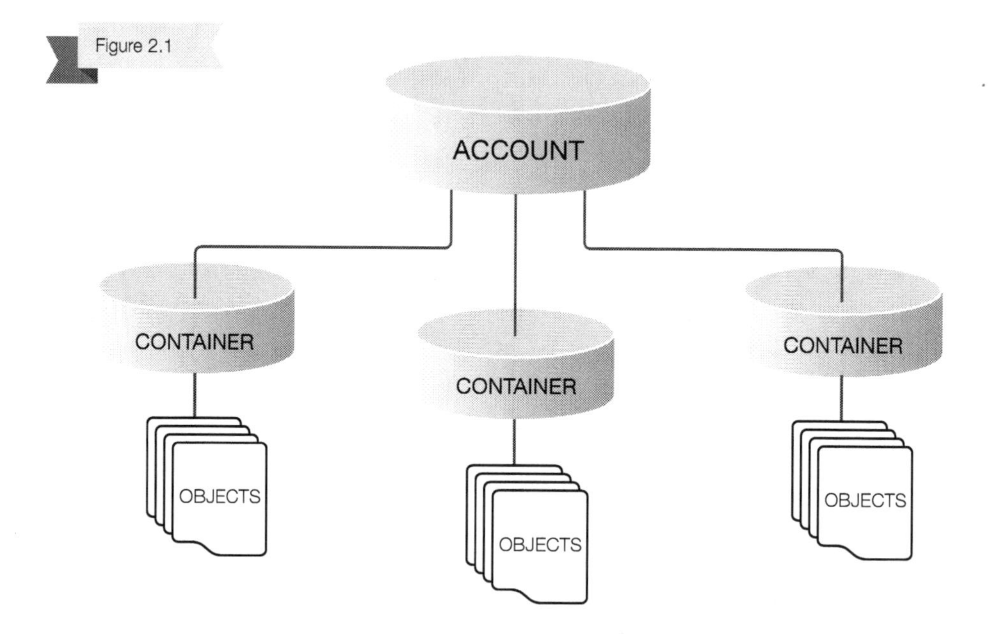

Objects

An object is the actual data is stored in Swift. This could include photos, videos or documents, log files, database backups, filesystem snapshots, or any other unstructured data.

The Swift API

Let's dig slightly deeper into the HTTP API. All uploads, downloads, and deleting happens by using HTTP verbs, such as PUT, GET, POST and DELETE.

To download an object, a 'GET' request would be made to the object's URL. A URL in Swift for an object looks like this:

```
https://swift.example.com/v1/account/container/object
```

To list all the objects in a container a 'GET' request would be made on a container:

```
https://swift.example.com/v1/account/container/
```

To get a list of all containers in an account, a 'GET' request would be made on the account:

```
https://swift.example.com/v1/account/
```

Uploading objects or creating containers are done with the 'PUT' HTTP verb. Updating metadata and additional features are enabled with the 'POST' verb. Naturally, deleting objects and containers is done with the 'DELETE' verb.

Applications can either communicate directly via the Swift API or use one of the many client libraries that exist for all popular programming languages, such as Java, Python, Ruby, and C#. The **`swift`** command-line client (CLI) and the SwiftStack Web Client also enable users to upload and manage their data in Swift via a simple interface.

Swift Architecture

So now that we understand the Swift URL, we can start to take a look at what is happening behind the URL. How does Swift translate that URL – with an account, container, and an object into the storage system?

The two basic components are the following. First, the proxy services, which route incoming requests to store or read data to the appropriate storage nodes. Next, the storage services, which store the actual data.

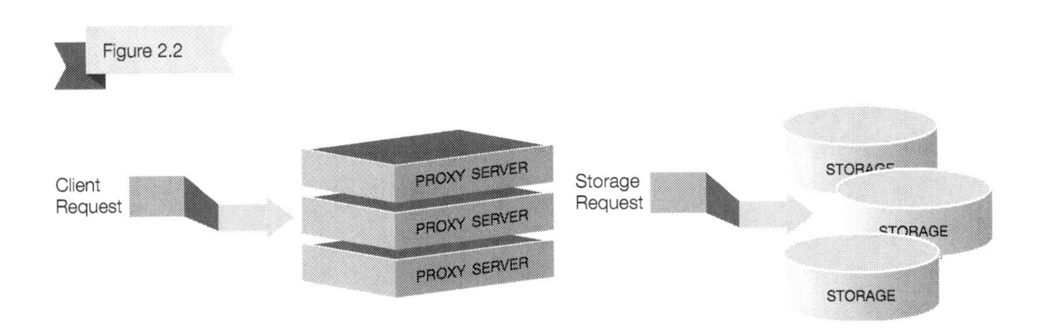

Figure 2.2

Proxy Server

The proxy servers are the public face of Swift and handle all incoming API requests. The proxy is an HTTP server that implements Swift's REST-ful API. As the only system in the Swift cluster that communicates with clients, the proxy is responsible for coordinating with the storage servers and replying to the client with appropriate messages. All messages to and from the proxy use standard HTTP verbs and response codes.

Once a proxy server receives a request, it will determine the storage node based on the URL of the object, for example *https://swift.example.com/v1/account/container/object.* The proxy server also coordinates responses, handles failures, and coordinates timestamps.

Proxy servers use a shared-nothing architecture and can be scaled as needed based on projected workloads. A minimum of two proxy servers should be deployed for redundancy. Should one proxy server fail, the others will take over.

When an object PUT request is made to Swift, the proxy server determines the correct storage nodes responsible for the data (based on a hash of the object name) and sends the object data to those object servers concurrently. If one of the primary storage nodes is unavailable, the proxy will choose an appropriate hand-off node to write data to. If a majority of the object servers respond with success, then the proxy returns success to the client.

Similarly, when an object GET request is made, the proxy determines which three storage nodes have the data and then requests the data from each node in turn. The proxy will return the object data from the first storage node to respond successfully.

Swift provides data durability by writing multiple – typically three – complete replicas of the data stored in the system. The proxy coordinates the read and write requests from clients and implements the read and write guarantees of the system. When a client sends a write request, the proxy ensures that the object has been successfully written to disk on the storage nodes before responding with a code indicating success.

Storage Servers

The Swift storage servers provide the on-disk storage for the cluster. There are three types of storage servers in Swift: account, container, and object.

Figure 2.3

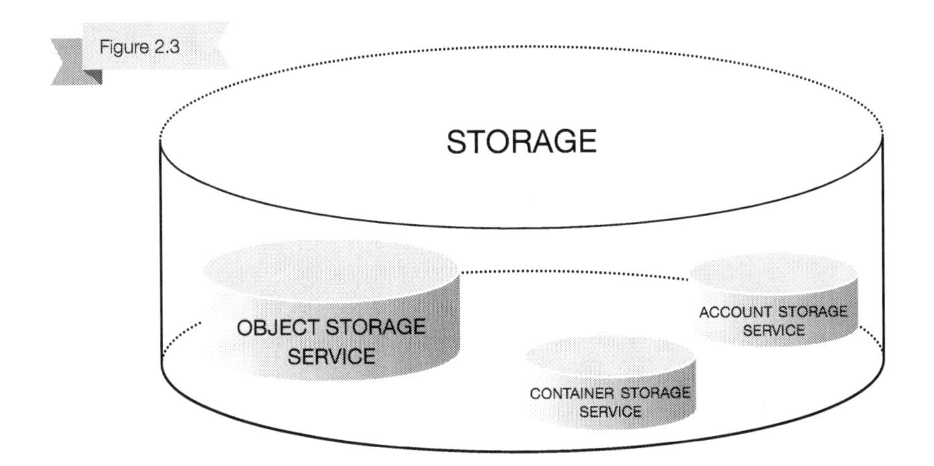

The account and container servers provide namespace partitioning and listing functionality. Additionally, the account server provides a listing of the containers within an account. They are implemented as SQlite databases on disk, and like all entities in Swift, they are replicated throughout the Swift cluster. An account database contains the list of containers in that account. Users are generally given access to a single Swift account within a cluster, and they have complete control over that unique namespace.

Object servers provide the on-disk storage for objects stored within Swift. Each object in Swift is stored as a single file on disk and object metadata is stored in the file's extended attributes. This simple design allows the object's data and metadata to be stored together and replicated as a single unit.

How Swift Works

Stitching it all together is the partition space. This partition space breaks up the storage available in the cluster into millions of 'locations' where data is located. Swift uses a data structure called the ring to map data to physical locations on disk. Then, replication processes ensure that data is replicated properly in each partition.

Partition Space

In Swift the partition space is used to store a collection of stored data, including either account databases, container databases, or objects. The partition space is core to the replication system. Think of a partition as a bin moving throughout a fulfillment center warehouse. Individual orders get thrown into the bin. The system treats that bin as a cohesive entity as it moves throughout the system. A bin full of things is easier to deal with than lots of little things. It makes for fewer moving parts throughout the system. As the system scales up, behavior continues to be predictable as the number of partitions remains fixed. The implementation of a partition is conceptually simple — a partition is just a directory sitting on a disk with a corresponding hash table of what it contains.

Swift partitions contain all data in the system.

Figure 2.4 **_The partition space is distributed across all available storage_**

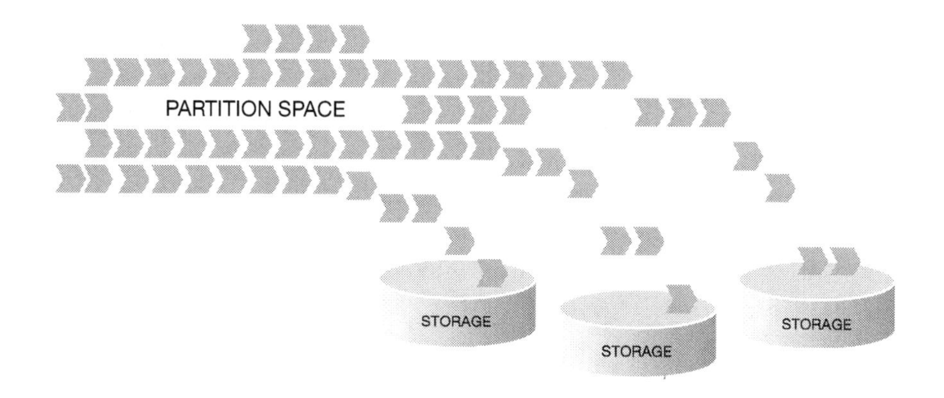

Figure 2.5 **_The relationship of a storage node, disk and a partition. Storage nodes have disks. Partitions are represented as directories on each disk_**

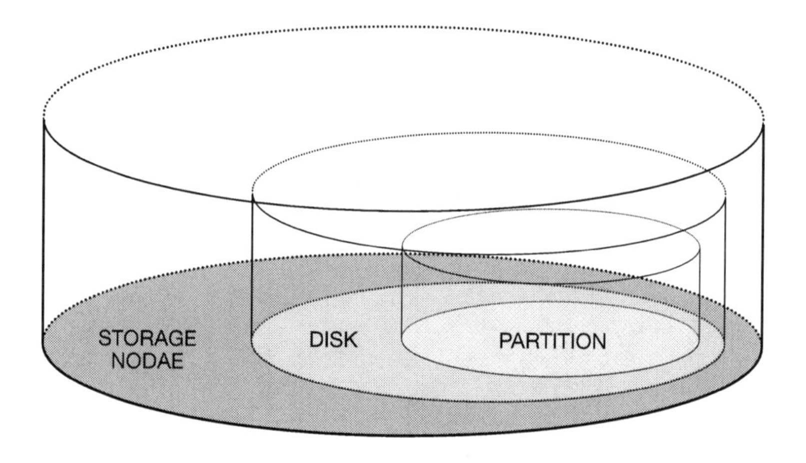

The Ring

The ring maps the partition space to physical locations on disk. When other components need to perform any operation on an object, container, or account, they need to interact with the ring to determine its location in the cluster. The ring maintains this mapping using zones, devices, partitions, and replicas.

Each partition in the ring is replicated three times by default across the cluster, and the locations for a partition are stored in the mapping maintained by the ring. The ring is also responsible for determining which devices are used for handoff should a failure occur.

Figure 2.6 ***The ring enables a path (/account/container/object) that is mapped to partitions***

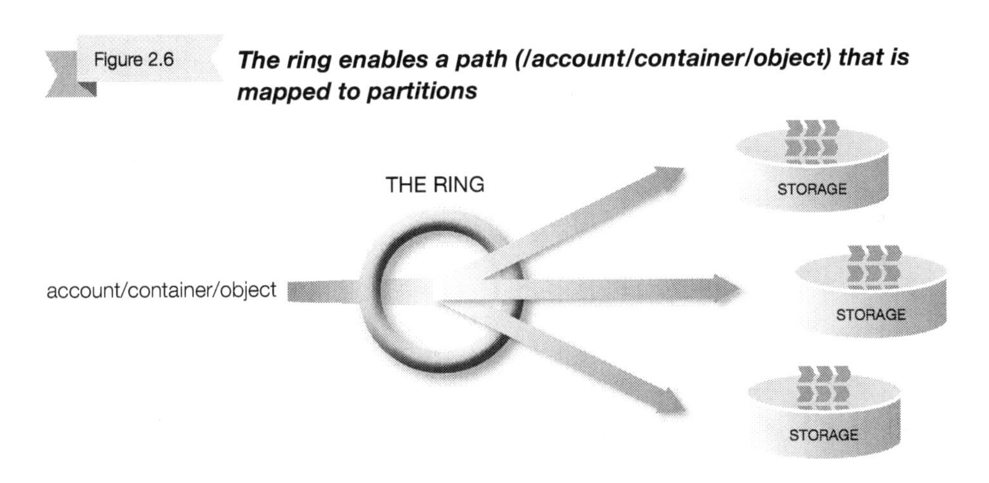

When new capacity is added, the partitions are rearranged and redistributed across the new available storage, taking with them the data. As a result, data becomes evenly distributed across the system.

Figure 2.7 ***New storage will receive a proportion of the existing partition space***

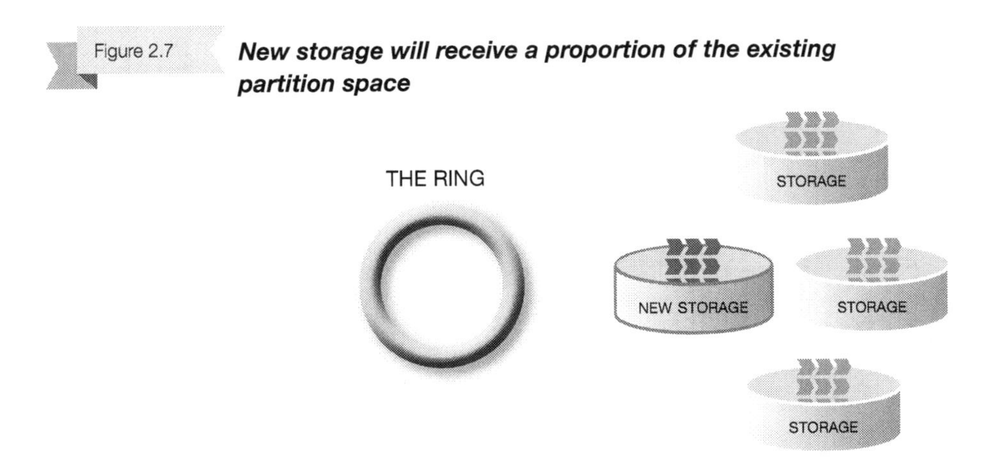

Consistency Servers

Storing data on disk and providing a REST-ful API to it is not hard. The hard part is handling failures. Swift's consistency servers are responsible for finding and correcting errors caused by both data corruption and hardware failures.

Auditors run in the background on every node in a Swift cluster and continually scan the disks to ensure that the data stored on disk has not suffered any bit-rot or file system corruption. If an error is found, the auditor moves the corrupted object to a quarantine area, and the replicators are responsible for replacing the data with a known-good copy.

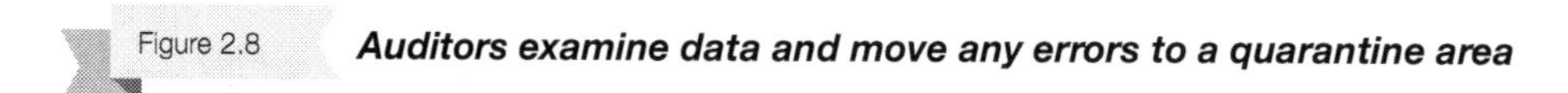

Figure 2.8 ***Auditors examine data and move any errors to a quarantine area***

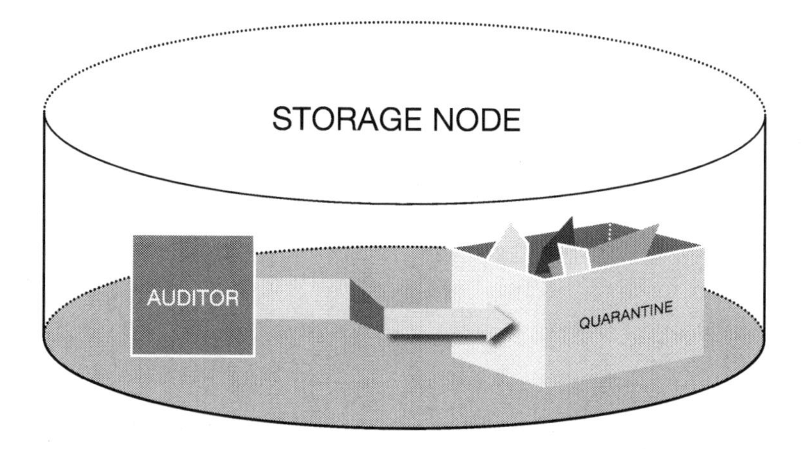

Updaters ensure that account and container listings are correct. The object updater is responsible for keeping the object listings in the containers correct, and the container updaters are responsible for keeping the account listings up-to-date. Additionally, the object updater updates the object count and bytes used in the container metadata, and the container updater updates the object count, container count, and bytes used in the account metadata.

Replicators ensure that the data stored in the cluster is where it should be and that enough copies of the data exist in the system. Generally, the replicators are responsible for repairing any corruption or degraded durability in the cluster. In order to ensure that there are three copies of the data everywhere, replicators continuously examine each partition. For each local partition, the replicator compares it against the replicated copies in the other Zones to see if there are any differences.

Figure 2.9 ***Replicators examine the checksums of partitions***

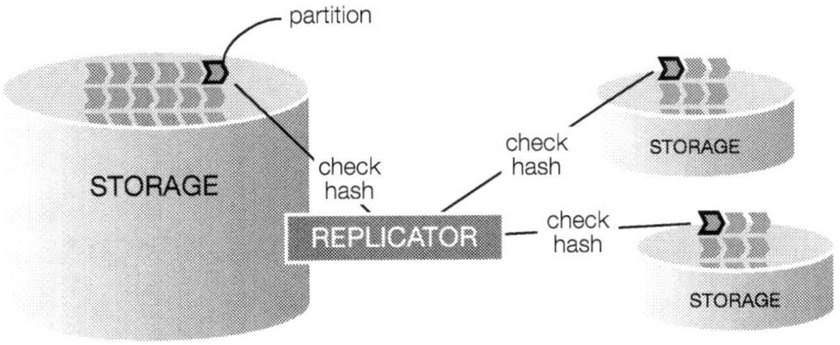

How does the replicator know if replication needs to take place? It does this by examining hashes. A hash file is created for each partition, which contains hashes of each directory in the partition. Each of the three hash files is compared. For a given partition, the hash files for each of the partition's copies are compared. If the hashes are different, then it is time to replicate and the directory that needs to be replicated is copied over.

This is where the partitions come in handy. With fewer "things" in the system, larger chunks of data are transferred around (rather than lots of little TCP connections, which is inefficient) and there are a consistent number of hashes to compare.

Zones

Swift allows availability zones to be configured to isolate failure boundaries. An availability zone is a distinct set of physical hardware with unique failure mode isolation. In a large deployment, availability zones may be defined as unique facilities in a large data center campus. In a single-DC deployment, the availability zones may be unique rooms, separated by firewalls and powered by different utility providers.

Figure 2.10 ***Storage can be placed in distinct fault-tolerant zones***

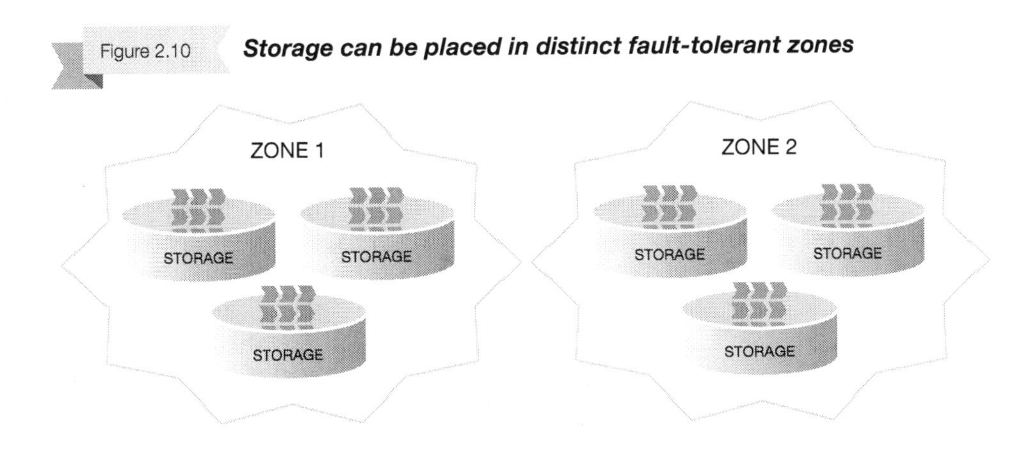

Regions

Swift lets you define regions when portions of the cluster may be placed in higher-latency, off-site locations. When a read request is made, the proxy node will favor 'nearby' copies of the data as measured by latency. When a write request is made, a durable write will happen locally, then replicas are transferred asynchronously to other regions.

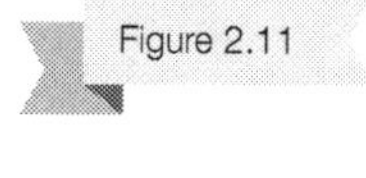

Figure 2.11 ***Storage zones can be deployed across geographic regions***

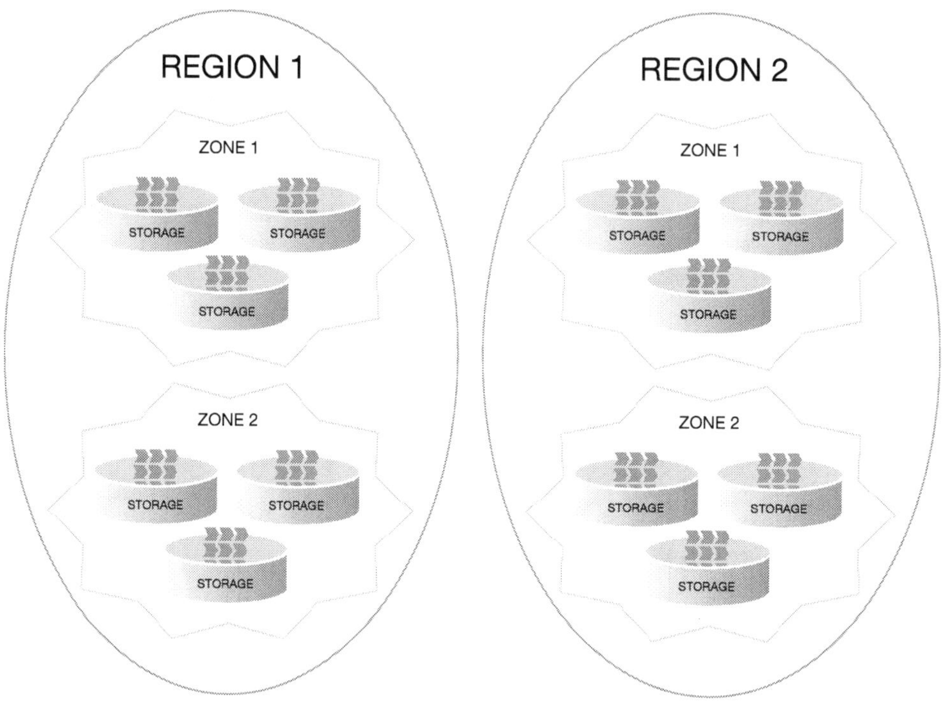

As unique as possible

One of the hard problems that needs to be solved in a distributed storage system is to figure out how to effectively place the data within the storage cluster. Swift has a "unique-as-possible" placement algorithm that ensures that the data is placed efficiently and with as much protection from hardware failure as possible.

When Swift was first released, deployers were required to have at least as many availability zones as replicas of their data. This data placement method did not work well for most deployments. Deployers were forced into convoluted deployment patterns that did not match their underlying hardware. Despite the actual details of the deployment, clusters were required to have at least three availability zones, and ideally four or five for handoff purposes. Often times this lack of deployment flexibility would cause deployers to do odd things. For example, a small cluster on two servers would be required to carve out some drives from each server to serve as a third availability zone.

Something better was needed, and so a better method was created. Swift's data placement method now uses "unique-as-possible" placement. With this new method, deployments are not required to force Swift's semantics onto a deployment that doesn't exactly match.

Swift's unique-as-possible placement works like this: data is placed into tiers – first the region, then zone, next the server, and finally the storage drive itself. When Swift chooses how to place each replica, it first will choose an availability zone that hasn't been used. If all availability zones have been chosen, the data will be placed on a unique server in the least used availability zone. Finally, if all servers in all availability zones have been used, then Swift will place replicas on unique drives on the servers.

The unique-as-possible placement gives deployers the flexibility to organize their infrastructure as they choose and configure Swift to take advantage of what has been deployed, without requiring that the deployer conform the hardware to the application running on that hardware.

Example Scenarios

To describe how these pieces all come together, let's walk through a couple of basic scenarios: uploading and downloading. These will help you understand more practically how Swift works.

Upload (PUT)

A client uses the RESTful API to make an HTTP request to PUT an object into an existing container. After receiving the PUT request, Swift determines where the data is going to go. To do this, the account name, container name, and object name are all used to determine the partition where this object should live. Then a lookup in the ring determines which storage nodes contain the partitions in question.

Then the data is sent to each storage node where it is placed in the appropriate partition. A quorum is required — at least two of the three writes must be successful before the client is notified that the upload was successful.

Figure 2.12 ***Quorum writes ensure durability***

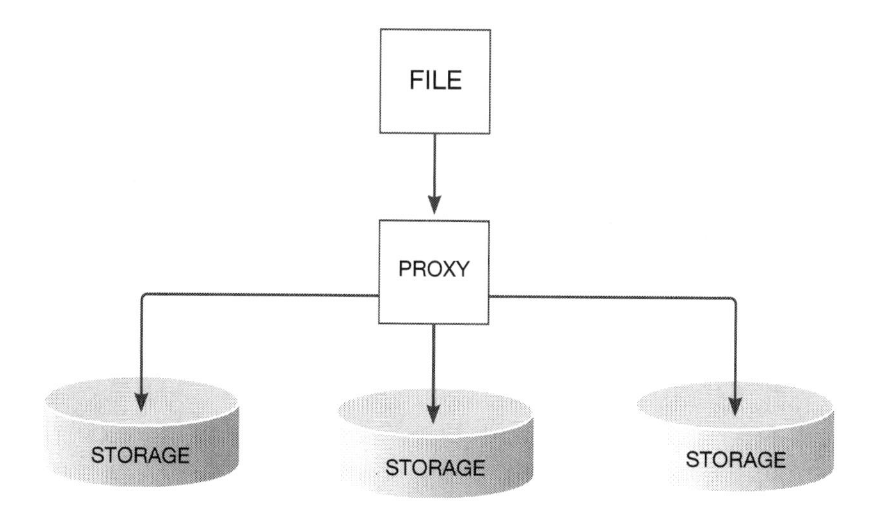

Next, the container database is updated asynchronously to reflect the new object in it.

Downloads (GET)

A request comes in for an account/container/object. Using the same consistent hashing, the partition name is generated. A lookup in the ring reveals which storage nodes contain that partition. A request is made to one of the storage nodes to fetch the object and if that fails, requests are made to the other nodes.

Figure 2.13 ***Get requests are handled by one of the storage nodes***

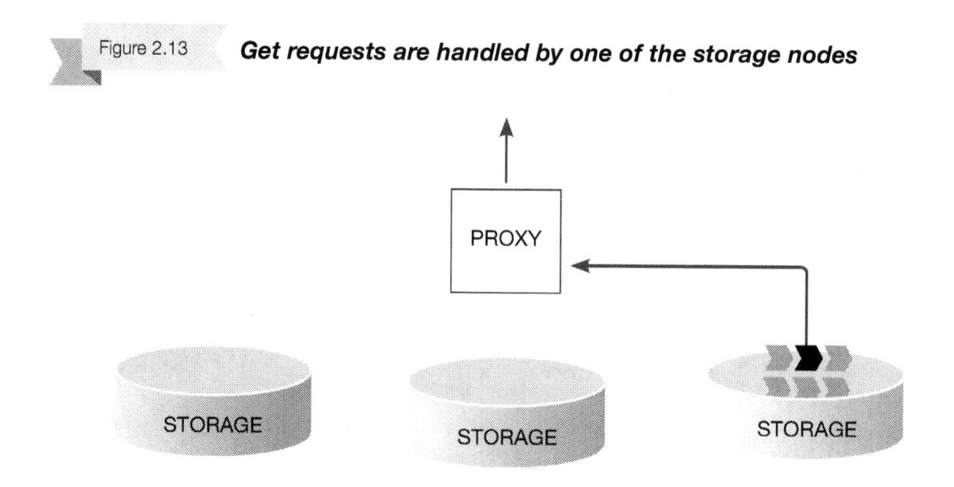

Conclusion

In this chapter you've become acquainted with the key concepts that Swift uses to organize, distribute, and serve data using:

- accounts and containers to create unique namespaces for objects
- proxy servers to route requests for reads and writes
- storage services for accounts, containers, and objects to store the data
- the partition space to store all the replicas for accounts, containers, and objects
- the ring to map partitions to physical locations
- and replicators, auditors, and updaters to keep everything consistent

You've also seen how these services come together to handle an upload and a download.

The next chapters cover these topics in much greater detail so that you can move from a conceptual understanding to becoming comfortable installing, operating, and maintaining Swift.

CHAPTER THREE

Using Swift

This chapter opens by demonstrating how to use the built-in **`swift`** command-line client to access Swift clusters. Next, we show how to develop applications using Swift's HTTP API (application programming interface). Then we introduce some advanced API features and middleware that allow you to develop more complex applications. Finally, we survey some client libraries that make it easier to write Swift applications in popular programming languages.

Command-Line Client

Most of the time, users and administrators access their Swift clusters using a client application. Swift clients can take many forms, from simple command-line tools to sophisticated GUI and web-based applications. We begin our exploration of Swift by looking at the **`swift`** command-line client, a simple but powerful tool that comes bundled with Swift.

Installation

Like all of the OpenStack clients, the **`swift`** client is a command-line interface (CLI) designed to be used from a command prompt. If you're not familiar with the command prompt, there are some great resources online to get you started, such as PeepCode's "Meet the command line" video (*https://peepcode.com/products/meet-the-command-line*).

The **`swift`** client comes bundled on your Swift nodes, but you can install it on any computer that can run Python. It is a Python program, but you don't need to know Python in order to use it. You do, however, need to have Python 2.6 or 2.7 installed on your system, along with a way of installing Python packages, such as `easy_install` or `pip`. Some operating systems come with these already installed, but if yours doesn't you'll need to install them, and that's a bit beyond the scope of what we can cover here. Consult the Python documentation (*http://docs.python.org/2/using/*) if you need help getting started.

The **`swift`** command–line client is packaged as `python-swiftclient`. Using the pip installer, a typical installation on Linux or OS X looks like:

```
$ sudo pip install python-swiftclient
```

If you run into trouble installing the **`swift`** command–line client, you can find more detailed installation instructions on the OpenStack website (*http://docs.openstack.org/cli/quick-start/content/install_clients.html*).

Authentication

Before you can access a Swift cluster with the command–line client, you need to authenticate, using three pieces of information:

- your Swift cluster's auth URL
- your username
- your password (or API key)

You can find the auth URL for your Swift cluster in the Cluster page of the SwiftStack Controller console:

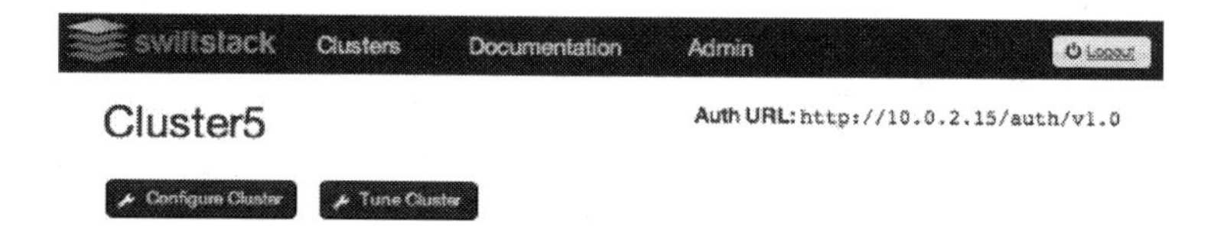

With an auth URL and user credentials, you can construct a **swift** command–line, like so:

```
$ swift -A <auth URL> -U <username> -K <password> <command>
```

We'll explain what to use for *<command>* in a moment, but for now the salient point is that you must pass your authentication credentials to the **swift** client. Since it would be cumbersome to provide these same parameters every time you execute a **swift** command, you can take advantage of some helpful environment variables to define your credentials just once per terminal session. In Linux and OS X, this looks like:

```
$ export ST_AUTH=<auth URL>
$ export ST_USER=<username>
$ export ST_KEY=<password>
```

Once you've set these environment variables, you no longer need to pass the credentials on the command line, simplifying your commands to:

```
$ swift <command>
```

For convenience, these environment variables can be set in a shell resource file, like `.bashrc` or `.zshrc`. Bear in mind that storing your Swift API key in a file like this might not be acceptable in more security-conscious environments.

Accessing Containers and Objects

Now that you know how to authenticate, you're ready to run swift commands against your cluster. The first thing you might like to do is see some basic information about the cluster, such as how many containers and objects you have in the cluster and how many bytes you're using. You can do this with the **stat** command:

```
$ swift stat
```

Account: AUTH_account

```
Containers: 2
Objects: 2
Bytes: 2048
```

You can get a listing of all the containers in the account with the **list** command:

```
$ swift list
animals
vegetables
```

Here you see that you have two containers. Create new containers with the **post** command:

```
$ swift post minerals
$ swift list
animals
minerals
vegetables
```

To get a listing of objects within a container, you can again use the **list** command, this time passing the container as a parameter:

```
$ swift list animals
lions.txt
tigers.txt
```

To upload objects to the cluster, you use the **upload** command, passing both the container and the object file name as parameters:

```
$ swift upload animals bears.txt
```

You can specify multiple files to upload in one command by passing additional parameters. If you specify a directory (folder) to upload instead of a file, all the files and directories within that directory will be uploaded, too.

Similarly, to download objects, use the **download** command, passing the container and object names as parameters:

```
$ swift download animals lions.txt
```

Finally, to remove an object from a container, use the **delete** command:

```
$ swift delete animals bears.txt
```

To remove a container and all the objects within it, pass only the container name:

```
$ swift delete animals
$ swift list
minerals
vegetables
```

As you can see, the **delete** command does not prompt for confirmation, and there is no way to restore objects once they have been deleted.

If you forget the commands available to you, running **swift** with no parameters will print a useful help message.

HTTP API

The **swift** command–line client is all you need to perform simple operations on your Swift cluster, but many users require more sophisticated client applications. Behind the scenes, all Swift applications, including the command–line client, use Swift's HTTP API to access the cluster, and that is the subject of this section.

Swift's HTTP API is RESTful, meaning that it exposes every container and object as a unique URL, and maps HTTP methods (like PUT, GET, POST, and DELETE) to the common data management operations (Create, Read, Update, and Destroy—collectively known as CRUD).

To see how the **swift** commands map to HTTP API calls, we'll repeat the examples from above, this time investigating the HTTP requests and responses at each step. And, as before, we start with authentication.

Authentication

Begin by making an HTTP request to the Swift authentication service to retrieve an auth token that can then be used to make authenticated requests to the Swift storage service. Assuming your Swift cluster has a domain name of, simply, "swift", your auth URL would be *https://swift/auth/v1.0* and the authentication request would look like this:

```
GET /auth/v1.0 HTTP/1.1
X-Auth-User: username
X-Auth-Key: password
```

You can see that the user credentials are passed in the `X-Auth-User` and `X-Auth-Key` request headers, and that they're passed in cleartext (not encrypted). Swift administrators can configure their clusters to use HTTPS, which will encrypt all communication between Swift clients and the cluster, ensuring that user credentials cannot be stolen and protecting the contents of objects stored in the cluster.

If you've supplied the correct credentials, Swift will respond with an auth token and a storage URL:

```
HTTP/1.1 200 OK
X-Storage-Url: https://swift/v1/AUTH_account
X-Auth-Token: AUTH_tk60217960bccf4c44b7d6baa98c77ce8d
Content-Length: 0
```

Note that the response has no content—all the salient information is returned in the response headers. The auth token, for example, is the value of the `X-Auth-Token` header. You will use the auth token and storage URL values in subsequent requests to the Swift cluster, so if you're writing a Swift application, you'll want to store those values in memory.

In most cases, we'll need to pass the auth token on every request. By default, Swift rejects unauthenticated requests with `HTTP 401 Unauthorized`, but we'll see in the Advanced API Features section (below) that Swift allows us to override the default permissions scheme with custom access control lists.

Auth tokens are valid for 24 hours, so you only have to authenticate once in every 24-hour period, and can use the same auth token in each request until it expires.

Accessing Containers and Objects

Now that you've authenticated, you can access the Swift storage service. You'll construct your URLs using the storage URL returned in the authentication response, and you'll pass the auth token as a request header.

As you might expect, you'll use the HTTP HEAD method to get status information from the cluster. You can retrieve usage statistics for the entire cluster by making a HEAD request to the storage URL alone:

```
HEAD /v1/AUTH_account HTTP/1.1
X-Auth-Token: AUTH_tk60217960bccf4c44b7d6baa98c77ce8d
```

Swift responds:

```
HTTP/1.1 204 No Content
Content-Length: 0
X-Account-Container-Count: 2
X-Account-Object-Count: 2
X-Account-Bytes-Used: 2048
```

As before, the salient information is contained in the response headers—the response body is empty. Here you can see how many containers and objects are in the cluster and how many bytes of storage have been used.

To list the containers in the account, you make a GET request to the storage URL:

```
GET /v1/AUTH_account HTTP/1.1
X-Auth-Token: AUTH_tk60217960bccf4c44b7d6baa98c77ce8d
```

Swift responds:

```
HTTP/1.1 200 OK
Content-Length: 19
X-Account-Container-Count: 2
X-Account-Object-Count: 2
X-Account-Bytes-Used: 2048

animals
vegetables
```

As before, Swift reports usage statistics in the response headers, but now the response also includes a list of container names in the response body.

If you want more information about the containers, such as how many objects they contain, we can use the `format=json` query string parameter:

```
GET /v1/AUTH_account?format=json HTTP/1.1
X-Auth-Token: AUTH_tk60217960bccf4c44b7d6baa98c77ce8d
```

The response now contains a JSON-formatted list of objects representing each container:

```
HTTP/1.1 200 OK
Content-Length: 96
X-Account-Container-Count: 2
X-Account-Object-Count: 2
X-Account-Bytes-Used: 2048

[{"count": 2, "bytes": 2048, "name": "animals"}, {"count": 0,
"bytes": 0, "name": "vegetables"}]
```

To create a container, you use the PUT HTTP method, appending the desired container name to the storage URL to form a new RESTful resource URL:

```
PUT /v1/AUTH_account/minerals HTTP/1.1
Content-Length: 0
X-Auth-Token: AUTH_tk60217960bccf4c44b7d6baa98c77ce8d
```

You may recall that you used the **swift post** command to create a container, but trust that the **swift** client is using the HTTP PUT method behind the scenes. That's because the **post** command is also used to update account, container, and object metadata, all of which, in Swift, use the HTTP POST method. When you use the **post** command to create a container, the **swift** client first tries to update the container metadata (POST), but falls back to creating the container (PUT) if it does not already exist.

To upload an object we again make a PUT request, this time appending the desired object name to the container's resource URL and passing the object content in the request body:

```
PUT /v1/AUTH_account/animals/bears.txt HTTP/1.1
Content-Length: 134
X-Auth-Token: AUTH_tk60217960bccf4c44b7d6baa98c77ce8d
Three Bears, once on a time, did dwell
Snug in a house together,
Which was their own, and suited well
By keeping out the weather.
```

Conversely, to retrieve an object, you make a GET request to the object's resource URL:

```
GET /v1/AUTH_account/animals/bears.txt HTTP/1.1
X-Auth-Token: AUTH_tk60217960bccf4c44b7d6baa98c77ce8d
```

Swift responds with the object content in the response body:

```
HTTP/1.1 200 OK
Content-Length: 134
Content-Type: text/plain
Three Bears, once on a time, did dwell
Snug in a house together,
Which was their own, and suited well
By keeping out the weather.
```

As you might expect, you can delete objects and empty containers with the HTTP DELETE method:

```
DELETE /v1/AUTH_account/animals/bears.txt HTTP/1.1
X-Auth-Token: AUTH_tkbbd137a67d1541ce857a712770b72487
```

The Swift HTTP API is richer than we've shown here, including support for pagination and result filtering. For a detailed description, consult the Swift API documentation (*http://docs.openstack.org/api/openstack-object-storage/1.0/content/index.html*). We'll demonstrate some more advanced API features in the next section.

Advanced API Features

In addition to the basic CRUD (Create/Read/Update/Delete) operations we've discussed thus far, the Swift API provides more advanced features that make it possible to build Swift applications that meet a variety of use cases.

Permissions and Access Control Lists (ACLs)

By default, Swift prevents unauthorized users from accessing objects that you've uploaded to your cluster. Only clients that provide an authentication token for your account can access objects that you've uploaded. That means that client applications must provide a valid auth token in the `X-Auth-Token` header on each request, and that the token must be associated with your storage account. When a client attempts to access a resource without the necessary authorization, Swift rejects the request with `HTTP 403 Forbidden`.

Sometimes you might want to allow other Swift users to access the objects and containers in your account. Other times you might want to give the general public (i.e., unauthenticated clients) access. In such cases, the Swift API allows you to define access control lists (ACLs) for containers and objects that define which users can access those containers and objects. For example, to give Goldilocks access to the ThreeBears container, you can use the **`swift post`** command:

```
$ swift post --read-acl goldilocks ThreeBears
```

Behind the scenes, the swift client POSTs to the Swift HTTP API, specifying the read ACL in the `X-Container-Read` request header:

```
POST /v1/AUTH_account/ThreeBears HTTP/1.1
Content-Length: 0
X-Auth-Token: AUTH_tkb9f3a661725b4db5b5848d499d5a09c3
```

```
X-Container-Read: goldilocks
```

The user *goldilocks* can now list and download the objects in your *ThreeBears* container. If you want *goldilocks* to be able to upload objects as well, you need to grant her write access by creating a write ACL:

```
$ swift post --write-acl goldilocks ThreeBears
```

As you might expect, the write ACL is specified in the `X-Container-Write` request header:

```
POST /v1/AUTH_account/ThreeBears HTTP/1.1
Content-Length: 0
X-Auth-Token: AUTH_tkb9f3a661725b4db5b5848d499d5a09c3
X-Container-Write: goldilocks
```

If you want to allow the general public (in other words, anyone who can access your Swift cluster using an HTTP client like a web browser) to download objects, you need to construct a read ACL granting access on the basis of the HTTP Referrer header instead of the Swift username:

```
$ swift post --read-acl '.referer:*, .rlistings' animals
```

Now unauthenticated users can list and download the objects in the *animals* container:

```
$ curl https://swift/v1/AUTH_account/animals
bears.txt
lions.txt
tigers.txt

$ curl https://swift/v1/AUTH_account/animals/bears.txt
Three Bears, once on a time, did dwell
Snug in a house together,
Which was their own, and suited well
By keeping out the weather.
```

The `.referrer` syntax is somewhat cryptic, so consult the ACL documentation (*http://docs.openstack.org/developer/swift/misc.html#module-swift.common.middleware.acl*) if you have a more complex use case. Note that Swift will not allow unauthenticated users to upload objects as write ACLs do not support the `.referrer` syntax.

Large Objects

Swift supports objects up to 5 GB in size, but many common use cases require the storage of files much larger than that. To upload large files, Swift applications must first split the files into 5 GB or smaller segments, upload them all to the same Swift container using a predictable naming pattern, and then link them all together with a special manifest object. The manifest object itself has no size, but defines an `X-Object-Manifest` header that specifies the naming pattern for the individual objects. Then, whenever a client downloads the manifest object, Swift concatenates all the objects that match the manifest's naming pattern and streams the result back to the user.

Fortunately, the **`swift`** command–line client handles segmentation of large objects for you. If you specify the `--segment-size` option when uploading an object, Swift will automatically divide the file into segments of the specified size, upload each one, and create a manifest file.

For example, you can upload a 12 GB file with the command:

```
$ swift upload --segment-size=5000000000 backups backup.zip
```

Behind the scenes, the **`swift`** client splits the file into three segments (5 GB + 5 GB + 2 GB), appends an ascending sequence number to each segment's name, uploads the three segments to the cluster, and then creates a *backup.zip* manifest object in the *backups* container.

```
source file                  object segments
                             backup.zip/00000000 (first 5 GB)
backup.zip (12 GB) ---->     backup.zip/00000001 (next 5 GB)
                             backup.zip/00000002 (last 2 GB)
```

You've learned how to upload objects previously, and uploading segments of a large object is no different. The new part here is the creation of the manifest file, which looks like this:

```
PUT /v1/AUTH_account/backups/backup.zip HTTP/1.1
Content-Length: 0
X-Object-Manifest: backups_segments/backup.zip
X-Auth-Token: AUTH_tkb9f3a661725b4db5b5848d499d5a09c3
```

There are a few interesting things to note here. First, the content length is zero. Manifests have no content, they are merely pointers to other objects in the cluster. Second, the `X-Object-Manifest` request header identifies this as a manifest object and defines the naming pattern for each of the large object's segments.

Finally, notice that the segment naming pattern is *backups_segments/backup.zip*. All objects in the *backups_segments* container with names beginning with *backup.zip* will be considered to be part of the *backup.zip* object and will be concatenated when that manifest object is downloaded.

If you followed this example carefully, you may have noticed that the **`swift`** client uploads segments to a special *<container>_segments* container, instead of to the container that stores the manifest. That's to avoid cluttering containers with lots of segments, but you can manually upload segments and manifests to the same container if you'd like. If you stick with the default and upload segments to their own container, and you intend to expose the manifest object to the general public using a read ACL as described in the previous section, then you must also grant access to the container housing the segments.

Object Versions

One of the common uses for a Swift cluster is storing backup files. Frequently, backup files are timestamped by appending a creation date to the filename. This way, new backup files don't overwrite old backup files, making it possible to restore to a previous back file if necessary. We say that backup files of this sort are versioned.

Swift has built-in support for object versioning.[1] Once you enable versioning on a container, every change to objects in that container will create a new version of the object.

To enable object versioning in a container, first you must create a new container to store the object versions, and then link the two containers by passing the `X-Versions-Location` header in a PUT request to the source container:

```
PUT /v1/AUTH_account/backups HTTP/1.1
X-Auth-Token: AUTH_tkbbd137a67d1541ce857a712770b72487
X-Versions-Location: backup_versions
```

Now, any time an object in the *backups* container is modified, a new version will be created and stored in the *backup_versions* container:

```
$ echo "the original file contents" > important.txt
$ swift upload backups important.txt
$ swift list backup_versions
```

1 The storage administrator must enable versioning support by setting `allow_versions` to `True` in `/etc/swift/container-server.conf` and restarting the container servers.

At this point, you'll see that the *backup_versions* container is empty. Now, make a change to the important file and upload it to the cluster:

```
$ echo "changes, for better or worse" >> important.txt
$ swift upload backups important.txt
$ swift list backup_versions
00dimportant.txt/1362713934.04880
```

Now you can see that the previous version of the important file has been stored in the *backup_versions* container. Swift uses a special naming scheme for versioned objects that includes the modification date as a UNIX timestamp. If you delete *important.txt* from the *backups* container, the most recent version will be restored:

```
$ swift delete backups important.txt
$ swift download --output - backups important.txt
the original file contents
```

Using the **download** command's `--output` option to print the object content directly to the terminal, you can see that the original file contents have been restored.

Expiring Objects

When dealing with temporary or time-sensitive data, you can let Swift manage object expiration for you by setting an expiration date or time-to-live on the object. To set an absolute expiration date, supply an `X-Delete-At` request header with the expiration date specified as a UNIX timestamp (seconds since midnight January 1st, 1970 GMT). To set a relative time-to-live, use the `X-Delete-After` header with the time-to-live specified in seconds. These headers can be used with PUT requests when creating new objects, or with POST requests to update existing objects.

Here's how you can create a new object that will expire in one hour (3600 seconds):

```
PUT /v1/AUTH_account/cache/hourly-report.csv HTTP/1.1
Content-Length: 65536
X-Auth-Token: AUTH_tkbbd137a67d1541ce857a712770b72487
X-Delete-After: 3600
```

Here's how you can update an existing object, setting it to expire at 2:14 AM EST on August 29, 1997:

```
POST /v1/AUTH_account/contracts/cyberdyne-systems.pdf HTTP/1.1
X-Auth-Token: AUTH_tkbbd137a67d1541ce857a712770b72487
X-Delete-At: 872838840
```

Once an object has reached its expiration time, Swift will reclaim the object's space and the object will no longer be available.

Custom metadata

By now you've seen a few examples of using Swift–specific metadata to control permissions, allow access to large objects, maintain object versions, and control object expiration. Swift also allows you to store your own custom metadata at the account, container, and object level. As before, metadata is set through the use of request headers, as described below.

Custom metadata takes the form of a key–value pair, where the key is used to construct the name of a request header, and the value becomes the value of that header. Metadata can be set with a PUT request when creating a container or object, or with a POST request when updating an account, container, or object.

The **`swift`** command–line client supports setting custom metadata with the --meta option to the **`post`** command:

```
$ swift post --meta Season:Winter images yosemite.jpg
```

This command sets the *Season* metadata key to the value of *Winter*. Swift does not care what metadata keys you use, or how many you define, so you're free to use any value that will fit into an HTTP header. Behind the scenes, the **`swift`** client constructs an `X-Object-Meta-Season` header and passes it in a POST request to update the object:

```
POST /v1/AUTH_account/images/yosemite.jpg HTTP/1.1
X-Object-Meta-Season: Winter
X-Auth-Token: AUTH_tkbbd137a67d1541ce857a712770b72487
```

Since you're updating an object here, you used a header of the form `X-Object-Meta-<key>`. If you were updating an account or a container you would use `X-Account-Meta-<key>` or `X-Container-Meta-<key>`, respectively.

You can view custom metadata with the stat command:

```
$ swift stat images yosemite.jpg
         Account: AUTH_account
       Container: images
          Object: yosemite.jpg
    Content Type: image/jpeg
  Content Length: 56124
     Meta Season: Winter
```

Behind the scenes, the **stat** command makes a HEAD request, as described earlier in the chapter.

To remove custom metadata, pass an empty string for the value of the key that you want to remove:

```
$ swift post --meta Season: images yosemite.jpg
```

This command sets the Season metadata key to an empty string, thus removing that key and any value that was previously defined.

Middleware

Administrators can enable middleware to add functionality to their Swift clusters.[2] The middleware components described here ship with SwiftStack, but it's also possible to install third-party middleware.

Static Web Server

With the ability to serve objects over HTTP, a Swift cluster acts almost like a static web server. By default, though, it's missing some basic web server functionality, namely the ability to serve directory index files and generate directory listings. The `staticweb` middleware adds these features, allowing a Swift cluster to be used as a simple static web server.

Once the `staticweb` middleware is enabled, Swift will use a container's metadata to determine whether to display an index file or generate a directory listing. To display index files (for example, index.html), set the `Web-Index` metadata key to the name of your index file:

```
$ swift post --meta Web-Index:index.html website
```

Now a request for `http://swift/v1/AUTH_account/website` will be translated internally to `http://swift/v1/AUTH_account/website/index.html`. Note that this requires an *index.html* object to exist in the *website* container.

If instead of serving an index file you want Swift to generate a nicely formatted

---

2 Usually this involves editing `/etc/swift/proxy-server.conf` and restarting the proxy servers, though SwiftStack provides a graphical user interface for managing middleware.

directory listing, you can set the `Web-Listings` metadata key to `TRUE`:

```
$ swift post --meta Web-Listings:TRUE images
```

Now a request for `http://swift/v1/AUTH_account/images` will display a nicely formatted directory listing. You can even control the CSS styles used to render the directory listing by pointing the `Web-Listings-CSS` metadata key to the name on a CSS file in the container.

Note that in order to use either `Web-Index` or `Web-Listings` with a container, that container must also have a read ACL that allows unauthenticated users to access the container, as described in the Permissions and Access Control Lists (ACLs) section (see above).

Temporary URLs

Sometimes you may want to allow unauthenticated clients to download specific objects, without granting public read access to an entire container. Furthermore, you may want to limit how long such users have access to these objects. That's where the `tempurl` middleware comes in. With it, application developers can write Swift applications that generate temporary URLs allowing users to download specific objects for a limited amount of time.

Temporary URLs are computed using a specific algorithm, defined in the documentation (*http://docs.openstack.org/trunk/openstack-object-storage/admin/content/swift-tempurl.html*) and they include a cryptographic signature and expiration date. In order to validate these secure URLs, the `tempurl` middleware requires that a secret key be defined on the account:

```
$ swift post --meta Temp-URL-Key opensesame
```

This command defines the `Temp-URL-Key` metadata, setting the secret key to *opensesame* and allowing the `tempurl` middleware to validate secure URLs.

Uploading Objects with HTML forms

When we covered permissions and access control lists (ACLs) previously, we said that container write access cannot be granted to unauthenticated users, i.e., the general public. But sometimes you may want web users to be able to upload objects to certain containers. For example, if you're building web–based collaboration software that allows users to share project files with each other, and you're using Swift to store the files on the back–end, you can allow users of the application to upload files directly to the Swift cluster even though they do not have Swift accounts.

The `formpost` middleware allows application developers to use standard HTML forms to upload new objects to a cluster. The middleware validates that the upload is allowed, using the same cryptographic signature method as the `tempurl` middleware, and then translates the POST request into separate PUT request for each uploaded file.

Cluster Hostname Mapping

The `domain_remap` middleware allows cluster administrators to rewrite storage URLs, moving the account or container name from the path into the hostname. The benefit of is this feature is to be able to use Swift as an origin for content distribution or caching by hostname. For example, with `domain_remap` enabled, you could write the URL:

```
http://swift/v1/AUTH_account/container/object
```

as:

```
http://auth-account.swift/container/object
```

or:

```
http://container.auth-account.swift/object
```

A setup like this generally requires wildcard DNS, which is outside the scope of this book. Note that underscores ("_") are mapped to dashes ("-"), because historically underscores have not been permitted in domain names.

Another middleware, `cname_lookup`, can be used in conjunction with `domain_remap` to provide friendly domain names that map directly to a specific account or container. This feature enables more concise hostname mappings that way more meaningful hostnames can be created. For example, *assets.example.com*. With `cname_lookup` enabled, Swift will use DNS to resolve the canonical name for any hostname that does not already end in the configured storage domain. That allows administrators to configure arbitrary domains that point to other accounts or containers. With our example *assets.example.com* could point to `container.auth-account.swift`.

Amazon Simple Storage Service (S3) API

Most of the time you will develop applications using the Swift HTTP API, or one of the language bindings that wrap it. But if you're working with third-party applications outside your control, you may need an alternative means of accessing the cluster.

The swift3 middleware, available through Github (*https://github.com/fujita/swift3*) implements Amazon's S3 API, allowing clients written for that specification to access a Swift cluster. While developed and distributed indepently of Swift proper, it is bundled with SwiftStack for convenience. Once enabled, your Swift containers will emulate Amazon S3 buckets.

Client Libraries

We've seen that Swift applications use the Swift HTTP API to access the cluster. Application developers can construct HTTP requests and parse HTTP responses using their programming language's HTTP client or they may choose to use open-source language bindings to abstract away the details of the HTTP interface.

Open–source client libraries are available for most modern programming languages, including:

- Python
- Ruby
- PHP
- C#/.NET
- Java

We'll cover the Python language bindings in some depth here, since they are bundled with the **`swift`** command–line tool described above. We'll follow that with a brief discussion of open-source client libraries available for the other languages.

Python

The Python language bindings are included in the `python-swiftclient` library mentioned earlier when we discussed the **`swift`** command–line client. Refer to the installation instructions in that section if you'd like to use this library.

You begin by importing the `swiftclient` module and instantiating a `Connection` object, passing your authentication credentials:

```
$ python
>>> from swiftclient import Connection
>>> conn = Connection(authurl='https://swift/auth/v1.0',
                      user='username', key='password')
```

You make requests to the cluster by invoking methods on the Connection Object. As you will see, the names of these methods are based on the underlying HTTP API calls. For example, to retrieve account metadata you would make an HTTP HEAD request to the account resource, which translates into invoking the `head_account` method:

```
>>> conn.head_account()
{
  'content-length': '0',
  'x-account-container-count': '2',
  'x-account-object-count': '2',
  'x-account-bytes-used': '2048'
}
```

As you can see, the `head_account` method returns a key–value dictionary of response headers. To retrieve a list of containers, you would make an HTTP GET request to the account resource, which translates into the `get_account` method—which, despite its name, gets containers, not accounts:

```
>>> headers, containers = conn.get_account()
>>> headers
{
  'content-length': '96',
  'x-account-container-count': '2',
  'x-account-object-count': '2',
  'x-account-bytes-used': '2048'
}
>>> containers
[{
  'count': 2,
  'bytes': 2048,
  'name': 'animals'
},
{
  'count': 0,
  'bytes': 0,
  'name': 'vegetables'
}]
```

The `get_account` method returns a tuple (an ordered list of elements) of two values: a dictionary of response headers, as before, and a list of dictionaries describing the containers in the cluster. Similarly, to list objects in a container, you call `get_container`, passing the container name as a parameter:

```
>>> headers, objects = conn.get_container('animals')
>>> headers
{
  'content-length': '477',
  'x-container-object-count': '2',
  'x-container-bytes-used': '2048'
}
>>> objects
[{
  'bytes': 1024,
  'last_modified': '2013-02-27T16:16:35.315280',
  'hash': '0f343b0931126a20f133d67c2b018a3b',
  'name': 'lions.txt',
  'content_type': 'text/plain'
},
{
  'bytes': 1024,
  'last_modified': '2013-02-27T16:16:35.323000',
  'hash': '0f343b0931126a20f133d67c2b018a3b',
  'name': 'tigers.txt',
  'content_type': 'text/plain'
}]
```

To upload an object, you call put_object, passing the container name, the desired object name, and the object contents as a file-like object:

```
>>> conn.put_object('animals', 'bears.txt', open('bears.txt'))
'f6036bba6d1ad119aca7b78a5b641432'
```

The `put_object` method returns the object's MD5 hash, which you can use to validate that the object stored in the cluster exactly matches the object on local disk.

As you might suspect, you retrieve an object with `get_object`:

```
>>> headers, contents = conn.get_object('animals', 'bears.txt')
>>> contents
Three Bears, once on a time, did dwell
Snug in a house together,
Which was their own, and suited well
By keeping out the weather.
```

The `swiftclient` library has more features than we've shown here, such as the ability to stream uploads and downloads of large objects, and to retry requests that fail. For more information, consult the API documentation (*http://docs.openstack.org/developer/python-swiftclient/*).

Ruby

The ruby-openstack library (*https://github.com/ruby-openstack/ruby-openstack*) provides Ruby language bindings for OpenStack Compute (Nova) and Object Storage (Swift), and supports v1 and v2 authentication schemes. Its object–oriented design lends method names that are more intuitive than `python-swiftclient's`. For example, here's how you would list objects in a container:

```
>> os = OpenStack::Connection.create(
   :auth_url => API_URL,
   :username => USERNAME,
   :api_key => API_KEY,
   :service_type => "object-store")
>> container = os.container('animals')
>> container.objects
=> ["lions.txt", "tigers.txt"]
```

PHP

Rackspace officially supports Swift in their new library, `php-opencloud` (*https://github.com/rackspace/php-opencloud*), which is currently undergoing active development. It has an object–oriented interface not unlike the `ruby-openstack` library described above. Here's how you would list objects in a container:

```
$ostore = $conn->ObjectStore();
$container = $ostore->Container('animals');
$objects = $container->ObjectList();
while($object = $objects->Next()) {
   printf("Object %s size=%u\n",
          $object->name, $object->bytes);
}
```

Rackspace's older `php-cloudfiles` library (*https://github.com/rackspace/php-cloudfiles*) also provides PHP bindings for Swift, but it has been deprecated and will not be updated after August 1, 2013.

C#/.NET

Similar to the PHP libraries described above, Rackspace provides two sets of C#/.NET language bindings for Swift. The first, `openstack.net` (*https://github.com/*

rackspace/openstack.net), is undergoing active development and does not yet support Swift, though that is planned.

The older `csharp-cloudfiles` project (*https://github.com/rackspace/csharp-cloudfiles*) supports Swift with an object–oriented interface similar to the Ruby and PHP libraries we looked at. Here's how to list objects in a container:

```
var creds = new UserCredentials("username", "password");
var client = new CF_Client();
var conn = new CF_Connection(creds, client);
var container = new CF_Container(conn, client, "animals");
var objects = container.GetObjectList(true);
foreach(var object in objects)
{
    Console.WriteLine(object["name"]);
}
```

Java

Several Java language bindings are available, but the jclouds library (*https://github.com/jclouds/jclouds*) seems to be the favorite. It supports OpenStack Swift and Nova and Amazon S3 object storage. Being Java, it tends to be more verbose than the libraries previously described. Here's how to list objects in a container:

```
BlobStoreContext context = ContextBuilder.newBuilder('swift')
  .endpoint("https://swift/auth/v1.0")
  .credentials('username', 'password')
  .buildView(BlobStoreContext.class);

RestContext<CommonSwiftClient,
          CommonSwiftAsyncClient> swift = context.unwrap();

PageSet<ObjectInfo> objects =
    swift.getApi().listObjects('animals');

for (ObjectInfo object : objects) {
    System.out.println(object.getName() + ": " +
          object.getBytes() + " bytes");
}
```

Conclusion

In this chapter, we've covered how to access a Swift cluster using the **`swift`** command–line tool and the HTTP API. We've also discussed some advanced API features and middleware options. We concluded our coverage of the API with a survey of client libraries for popular programming languages. In the chapters that follow, you'll learn how to install (Chapter 4), use the SwiftStack Controller (Chapter 5), set up (Chapter 6), and operate (Chapter 7) a Swift cluster.

CHAPTER FOUR

Installing OpenStack Swift

Once you've decided to try OpenStack Swift, you'll need to understand how to configure and deploy your cluster. There are many configuration options and installation decisions to make. In this chapter you'll learn the details of how to get a Swift cluster up and running, exploring each core configuration option.

We will do this by first covering the download and installation of OpenStack Swift direct from source and go into detail about the configuration options (Part I). This will provide a foundation for understanding any automation tools that you may use when doing a deployment.

While there are many ways to proceed through each step, we will note where there are potential landmines, so you can learn from our experiences.

Later in the chapter (Part II), we cover how to install a SwiftStack node which can serve as a point of comparison for how to automate OpenStack Swift installation.

Part I

Downloading OpenStack Swift

The official releases are available on GitHub at *https://github.com/openstack/swift.*

For each major release of OpenStack there is a version of Swift.

SwiftStack always recommends deploying and staying current with the latest released version of OpenStack Swift. Swift has a frequent release schedule. You can see which versions of Swift have been tagged for release at *https://github.com/openstack/swift/tags*. Swift releases are numbered, for example '1.8.0'.

To install from source:

```
$ sudo apt-get install git python-setuptools
$ cd /opt
$ git clone git://github.com/openstack/swift.git
$ cd swift
$ sudo python setup.py install
```

To prepare configuration files:

```
$ sudo mkdir -p /etc/swift
$ cd /opt/swift/etc
$ cp account-server.conf-sample /etc/swift/account-server.conf
$ cp container-server.conf-sample /etc/swift/container-server.conf
$ cp object-server.conf-sample /etc/swift/object-server.conf
$ cp proxy-server.conf-sample /etc/swift/proxy-server.conf
$ cp drive-audit.conf-sample /etc/swift/drive-audit.conf
$ cp swift.conf-sample /etc/swift/swift.conf
```

Depending on your distribution there may be some dependencies needed for your system. For example, on Ubuntu, you may need to `apt-get` install the following packages:

gcc
bzr
python-configobj
python-coverage
python-dev
python-nose
python-setuptools
python-simplejson
python-xattr
python-webob
python-eventlet
python-greenlet
debhelper
python-sphinx
python-all

python-openssl
python-pastedeploy
python-netifaces
bzr-builddeb
xfsprogs
memcached

With Ubuntu, the command would be:

```
$ sudo apt-get install gcc bzr python-configobj python-coverage python-dev python-nose python-setuptools python-simplejson python-xattr python-webob python-eventlet python-greenlet debhelper python-sphinx python-all python-openssl python-pastedeploy python-netifaces bzr-builddeb xfsprogs memcached
```

At this point, you should be able to run

```
$ swift-init
```

This command is similar to 'service' or 'start|stop' in that you can start/stop/reload Swift processes.

Ensure that the command can run, but don't expect it to start Swift up quite yet. There is still configuration that needs to be done, which is the topic of the rest of this chapter.

SwiftStack will install all prerequisite packages; the latest tested version of OpenStack Swift; and Swift will be automatically kept up-to-date with the latest versions. A SwiftStack Node install will be covered later in this chapter.

Preparing the Drives

Storing data on hard drives is why we're here, so let's start with formatting a drive. Also keep in mind through this process that there is no RAID used as data is copied wholly to multiple drives in the system.

You'll need a system with disks, naturally! We will also need to install `xfsprogs`. For example, on Ubuntu, this would be:

```
$ sudo apt-get install xfsprogs
```

Survey What's on the System

First you need to identify what drives you have, what drives on the node should be formatted, and which ones are system drives that shouldn't be formatted. Run:

```
$ df
Filesystem     1K-blocks      Used  Available  Use%  Mounted on
/dev/sda1       27689156   8068144   18214448   31%  /
none             1536448       672    1535776    1%  /dev
none             1543072      1552    1541520    1%  dev/shm
none             1543072        92    1542980    1%  /var/run
none             1543072         0    1543072    0%  /var/lock
```

This should list all mounted filesystems. Just note which device is used for booting so you don't accidentally format it later.

This is likely the `sda` device mounted on /. But we can can prove it to ourselves by poking around in */proc/mounts*. See how the `rootfs` is listed here:

```
$ cat /proc/mounts
rootfs / rootfs rw 0 0
none /sys sysfs rw,nosuid,nodev,noexec,relatime 0 0
none /proc proc rw,nosuid,nodev,noexec,relatime 0 0
none /dev devtmpfs
rw,relatime,size=1536448k,nr_inodes=211534,mode=755 0 0
none /dev/pts devpts
rw,nosuid,noexec,relatime,gid=5,mode=620,ptmxmode=000 0 0
fusectl /sys/fs/fuse/connections fusectl rw,relatime 0 0
/dev/disk/by-uuid/c9402f9d-30ed-41f2-8255-d32bdb7fb7c2 / ext4
rw,relatime,errors=remount-ro,commit=600,barrier=1,data=ordered 0 0
none /sys/kernel/debug debugfs rw,relatime 0 0
none /sys/kernel/security securityfs rw,relatime 0 0
none /dev/shm tmpfs rw,nosuid,nodev,relatime 0 0
none /var/run tmpfs rw,nosuid,relatime,mode=755 0 0
none /var/lock tmpfs rw,nosuid,nodev,noexec,relatime 0 0
binfmt_misc /proc/sys/fs/binfmt_misc binfmt_misc
rw,nosuid,nodev,noexec,relatime 0 0
gvfs-fuse-daemon /home/joe/.gvfs fuse.gvfs-fuse-daemon
rw,nosuid,nodev,relatime,user_id=1000,group_id=1000 0 0
```

To find out what other block devices the operating system knows about look in the directory */sys/block*.

This should list all the block devices that are known on the system.

```
$ ls /sys/block
$ ls
loop0 loop3 loop6 ram1  ram12 ram15 ram3 ram6 sda sdd sdg sdj sdm
loop1 loop4 loop7 ram10 ram13 ram19 ram4 ram7 sdb sde sdh sdk
loop2 loop5 ram0  ram11 ram14 ram2  ram5 ram8 sdc sdf sdi sdl
```

The devices you're interested in are the ones starting with *sd*, but other systems may have different prefixes.

Also review which filesystems are formatted by running the following, which you may need to run as root.

```
$ sudo blkid
/dev/sda1: UUID="c9402f9d-30ed-41f2-8255-d32bdb7fb7c2" TYPE="ext4"
/dev/sda5: UUID="b2c9d42b-e7ae-4987-8e12-8743ced6bd5e" TYPE="swap"
```

With the output of these, you can start building up a list of devices that the system knows about that need to be formatted. Identify all the devices in */sys/bock* that are not formatted (or not formatted in the manner specified here) and run.

```
$ sudo mkfs.xfs -f -i size=512 -L d1 /dev/sdb
...and the next drive
$ sudo mkfs.xfs -f -i size=512 -L d2 /dev/sdc
...and so on
$ sudo mkfs.xfs -f -i size=512 -L d3 /dev/sdd
```

Swift uses extended attributes, so be sure to set the default inode block size to something larger than the default. SwiftStack recommends 512 for most applications.

Notice what we didn't create device partitions. Partitioning is unnecessary abstraction for Swift because you're going to use the entire device.

It's important to label each device. During operations, device 'letter names' may change if devices are added or removed and the system is rebooted. For example, */dev/sdr* may become */dev/sds*. By labeling each device you can keep an inventory of each device in the system and properly mount the device. The strategy the SwiftStack Node software uses is to create and inventory a universally unique identifier (UUID) for each device.

Mounting

The next step is to tell the operating system to attach the `xfs` filesystems on the devices you just created somewhere so that Swift can find them and start putting data on them.

Create a directory in */srv/node/* for a place to mount the filesystem.

It's nice to be able map devices to directories for where the device is to be mounted.

So let's use the label as a directory name that we can then use to mount the filesystem.

```
$ sudo mkdir -p /srv/node/d1
$ sudo mkdir -p /srv/node/d2
...
```

For each drive you wish to mount, type

```
$ sudo mount -t xfs -o noatime,nodiratime,logbufs=8 -L d1 \
    srv/node/d1
$ sudo mount -t xfs -o noatime,nodiratime,logbufs=8 -L d2 \
    srv/node/d2
```

and so on...

After the drives are mounted, a user needs to be created that has read-write permissions to the directories where the devices have been mounted. The default user that Swift uses is the user 'swift'. To create the user run the command:

```
$ sudo useradd swift
```

Next the user 'swift' needs to be given permission to the directories. Run the command:

```
$ chown -R swift:swift /srv/node
```

Right now we're running these commands by hand; this means that nobody is going to be running them the next time the machine reboots, but you'd need to before swift tries to startup.

To do this you need to create a script that contains each one of those 'mount' commands you just ran and place it in */opt/swift/bin/mount_devices*.

```
$ mount -t xfs -o noatime,nodiratime,logbufs=8 -L d1 /srv/node/d1
$ mount -t xfs -o noatime,nodiratime,logbufs=8 -L d2 /srv/node/d2
...
$ mount -t xfs -o noatime,nodiratime,logbufs=8 -L d36 /srv/node/d36
```

Next create an upstart script in */etc/init/start_swift.conf.*

```
description "mount swift drives"
start on runlevel [234]
stop on runlevel [0156]
exec /opt/swift/bin/mount_devices
```

Be sure to test this out by rebooting the system.

```
$ sudo reboot
```

And to make sure that it was mounted properly with all the configuration settings type:

```
$ mount
/dev/sda1 on / type ext4 (rw,errors=remount-ro, commit=0)
proc on /proc type proc (rw,noexec,nosuid,nodev)
none on /sys type sysfs (rw,noexec,nosuid,nodev)
fusectl on /sys/fs/fuse/connections type fusectl (rw)
none on /sys/kernel/debug type debugfs (rw)
none on /sys/kernel/security type securityfs (rw)
none on /dev type devtmpfs (rw,mode=0755)
none on /dev/pts type devpts (rw,noexec,nosuid,gid=5,-
   mode=0620)
none on /dev/shm type tmpfs (rw,nosuid,nodev)
none on /var/run type tmpfs (rw,nosuid,mode=0755)
none on /var/lock type tmpfs (rw,noexec,nosuid,nodev)
binfmt_misc on /proc/sys/fs/binfmt_misc type binfmt_misc
   (rw,noexec,nosuid,nodev)
/dev/sdc1 on /srv/node/sdc type xfs (rw,noatime,nodira-
   time,nobarrier,logbufs=8)
```

Labeling Devices

Keep in mind a system reboot scenario. It's important to keep track of which devices need to be mounted to which system location. This can be done with mounting by labels in a separate upstart script created for Swift. Labeling the disk will give the disk the same device name when the OS reboots. If you don't do this, then the next time the OS boots, it may come up under a different device name. This would lead to all sorts of unexpected behaviors when the cluster reboots.

SwiftStack recommends not using `fstab` for this purpose. `fstab` is used to automatically mount filesystems upon boot time. Make sure that the only items listed in here are critical for the booting of the machine, because the machine may hang on boot time if it can't mount a device. This is likely when running a big box full of disks.

The above example is a standard configuration location to mount devices in swift. The default is */srv/node*, but you can mount them anywhere.

To change the location, update the configuration setting in the following configuration files:

'devices' in the configuration files 'account-server.conf', 'container-server.conf', 'object-server.conf'
'device_dir' in drive-audit.conf
and
'path' in rsyncd.conf

Nobarrier
Unless you know what you're doing, do not use 'nobarrier'. See *http://xfs.org/index.php/XFS_FAQ#Write_barrier_support* for more details.

Creating the Rings: Builder Files

The rings map the location for every bit of data in the cluster. It's the data structure that enables Swift to replicate data across all the drives in the cluster. Drives are error prone (even SSDs), so Swift is designed to store multiple copies of data throughout the system. In fact, we're going to specify that right now, so it's a good idea to learn how this works.

The primary goal here is not only to explain how to run a few important commands, but also to help you really understand how Swift works. This will make you better informed while building your cluster.

First let's create the builder files:

```
$ cd /etc/swift
$ sudo swift-ring-builder account.builder create 18 3 24
$ sudo swift-ring-builder container.builder create 18 3 24
$ sudo swift-ring-builder object.builder create 18 3 24
```

Such a critical configuration component needs some breaking down.

Mechanics of Creating Builder Files

Let's go back to the `swift-ring-builder` command and take a closer look at its options.

If we run:

```
$ swift-ring-builder
swift-ring-builder 1.3

swift-ring-builder <builder_file>
```

We see information about the ring and the devices within.

```
swift-ring-builder <builder_file> add
   z<zone>-<ip>:<port>/<device_name>_<meta> <weight>
   [z<zone>-<ip>:<port>/<device_name>_<meta> <weight>] ...
```

Adds devices to the ring with the given information. No partitions will be assigned to the new device until after running 'rebalance'. This is so you can make multiple device changes and rebalance them only once.

```
swift-ring-builder <builder_file> create <part_power> <repli-
   cas>
                                          <min_part_hours>
Creates <builder_file> with 2^<part_power> partitions and
   <replicas>.
<min_part_hours> is number of hours to restrict moving a par-
   tition more than once.
swift-ring-builder <builder_file> list_parts <search-value>
   [<search-value>] ..
```

Returns a 2 column list of all the partitions that are assigned to any of the devices matching the search values given. The first column is the assigned partition number and the second column is the number of device matches for that partition. The list is ordered from most number of matches to least. If there are a lot of devices to match against, this command could take a while to run.

```
swift-ring-builder <builder_file> rebalance
```

Attempts to rebalance the ring by reassigning partitions that haven't been recently reassigned.

```
swift-ring-builder <builder_file> remove <search-value>
   [search-value ...]
```

Removes the device(s) from the ring. This should normally just be used for a device that has failed. For a device you wish to decommission, it's best to set its weight to 0, wait for it to drain all its data, then use this remove command. This will not take effect until after running 'rebalance.'This is so you can make multiple device changes and rebalance them only once.

```
swift-ring-builder <builder_file> search <search-value>
```
Shows information about matching devices.

```
swift-ring-builder <builder_file> set_info
    <search-value> <ip>:<port>/<device_name>_<meta>
    [<search-value> <ip>:<port>/<device_name>_<meta>] ...
```
For each search-value, resets the matched device's information. This information isn't used to assign partitions, so you can use write_ring afterward to rewrite the current ring with the newer device information. Any of the parts are optional in the final <ip>:<port>/<device_name>_<meta> parameter; just give what you want to change. For instance set_info d74 _"snet: 5.6.7.8" would just update the meta data for device id 74.

```
swift-ring-builder <builder_file> set_min_part_hours <hours>
```
Changes the <min_part_hours> to the given <hours>. This should be set to however long a full replication/update cycle takes. We're working on a way to determine this more easily than scanning logs.

```
swift-ring-builder <builder_file> set_weight <search-value>
    <weight>
    [<search-value> <weight] ...
```
Resets the devices' weights. No partitions will be reassigned to or from the device until after running 'rebalance'. This is so you can make multiple device changes and rebalance them only once.

```
swift-ring-builder <builder_file> validate
```
Just runs the validation routines on the ring.

```
swift-ring-builder <builder_file> write_ring
```
This rewrites the distributable ring file. It is done automatically after a successful rebalance, so really this is only useful after one or more 'set_info' calls when no rebalance is needed but you want to send out the new device information.

The <search-value> can be of the form:

```
d<device_id>z<zone>-<ip>:<port>/<device_name>_<meta>
```

Any part is optional, but you must include at least one part.

Examples:

```
d74 Matches the device id 74
z1  Matches devices in zone 1
z1-1.2.3.4    Matches devices in zone 1 with the ip 1.2.3.4
1.2.3.4       Matches devices in any zone with the ip 1.2.3.4
z1:5678       Matches devices in zone 1 using port 5678
:5678         Matches devices that use port 5678
/sdb1         Matches devices with the device name sdb1
_shiny        Matches devices with shiny in the meta data
_"snet: 5.6.7.8" Matches devices with snet: 5.6.7.8 in the
   meta data
[::1]         Matches devices in any zone with the ip ::1
z1-[::1]:5678 Matches devices in zone 1 with ip ::1 and port
   5678
```

Most specific example:

```
d74z1-1.2.3.4:5678/sdb1_"snet: 5.6.7.8"
```

Nerd explanation:
All items require their single character prefix except the ip, in which case the - is optional unless the device id or zone is also included.

Quick list: `add create list_parts rebalance remove search set_info set_min_part_hours set_weight validate write_ring`

Exit codes:
```
0 = operation successful
1 = operation completed with warnings
2 = error
```

It should spew out a bunch of options: the one we're interested in is `create`, so to see the `create` options, run:

```
$ swift-ring-builder account.builder create
```

The format of the `create` command is:

```
swift-ring-builder (account|container|object).builder create
    <part_power> <replicas> <min_part_hours>
```

When we run the command `create` the builders files are created.

Builder Files

Think of the builder file as a big database. It contains a record of all the storage servers and storage devices in the cluster.

For each 'thing' we store in the Swift cluster, we'll need a builder file to map those 'things' back to physical locations in the storage cluster.

The cluster stores:

1. Accounts
2. Containers
3. Objects

Each account has the data for all the containers for that account. Each container also has the data for all the objects in that container. Finally, there are the objects themselves.

So the commands we will be running are:

```
swift-ring-builder account.builder create <part_power> <rep-
    licas> <min_part_hours>
swift-ring-builder container.builder create <part_power>
    <replicas> <min_part_hours>
swift-ring-builder object.builder create <part_power> <repli-
    cas> <min_part_hours>
```

The three parameters the 'create' command takes are:

'part_power' which determines the number of partitions created storage cluster.
'repliacas' specify how many replicas you would like stored in the cluster.
'min_part_hours' specifies the frequency at which a replica is allowed to be moved.

Let's dig a bit deeper into each of these configuration settings.

Partitions

Partitions are the buckets that data goes into. This deserves some explanation as it is core to a functioning replication system.

Think of a partition as a bin. Lots of things get thrown into this bin. The system treats that bin as a cohesive entity as it is placed throughout the system. A fixed number of bins is easier to deal with than lots of individual files because it makes for fewer moving parts throughout the system.

So when it's said that "data" is replicated "three times," what's replicated is a partition.

The way that partitions works with Swift is that they reduce the number of things that are in the system. To get this predictable behavior, the partitions are actually fixed in number throughout the system. You determine the number of partitions when you configure your cluster. This leads to more predictable system behavior as partitions doesn't change dynamically.

The implementation of a partition is conceptually simple – a partition is just a directory sitting on disk somewhere – wherever the ring says it should live.

'part_power'

Partitions must be set when creating the builder files. So your first thought might be to choose a very large number. However, replication may take longer in that scenario because files can't be grouped together for replication checks or rsyncing. Also, lookups take a fraction longer because the ring gets that much bigger. Lastly, larger partitions means it takes longer to build the ring when making future changes.

Remember a partition is just a directory on disk somewhere. So what is being considered is how many partitions will live on each disk and the total number of disks that you expect for the system to have.

For the purposes of configuration, the ring builder asks for the 'part_power', which means that the number partitions will be 2^part_power.

To determine the number of partitions to create, here is a rule of thumb formula:

100 partitions x the maximum number of drives that you think you will ever have in the cluster, rounded up to the nearest power of 2.

For example, on a large deployment done with 1,800 drives, the plan was to grow the cluster size by an order-of-magnitude. That would come out to be (1,800 * 10 * 100) 1,800,000 partitions. The nearest power of 2 for 1,800,000 is 2^21 which is 2,097,152. So the 'part_power' was set to 21.

When choosing the top-end of number of disks for the lifetime of the system consider the physical, size limitations of the deployment. How big is the data center space allocated for this cluster? How much power can be supplied? Even if you guess wrong, there is still recourse – it's always possible to stand up another object storage cluster and have the authentication system route new accounts to that new storage cluster.

When you choose your 'part_power' number, this will be used in the ring builder 'create' command.

Why you Never Want to Change the Number of Partitions

If you do need to change the number of partitions in the ring, here is what happens. The data isn't gone, it will just have to reshuffle every single thing in the cluster. The data will be inaccessible for some period of time before the system is repartitioned and the data is where it should be. So if at all possible you'll want to avoid needing to change the number of partitions.

SwiftStack has strategies for changing part-power for SwiftStack deployments to ensure that this limitation is not hit.

Replicas

The replica count can be set with this configuration setting which impacts the system durability, availability, and the amount of disk space used. SwiftStack recommends using 3 replicas.

Durability is calculated by determining the odds of 3 partitions residing on drives across the system becoming corrupt (or otherwise failing) before the continuously running replication/auditing processes notice and push data to handoff locations. With Swift, if a drive fails, the entire cluster will participate in replicating data to handoff locations, which dramatically reduces the MTTR (mean time to repair) compared with standard 3-way mirroring or RAID.

SwiftStack recommends using the value 3 when setting 'replicas' in the ring builder 'create' command.

Min Part Hours

The minimum part hours (`min part hours`) setting ensures that only one partition's replica is moved at a time. If multiple replicas are in flight at the same time, there is a risk that data may become inaccessible. By setting `min part hours` to something greater than what it takes for the system to do a full partition replication cycle, it gives the system enough time for replications to happen – one at a time.

A good default setting is 24 hours. To tune, look at the logs of each replicator on each object store. In the log it will say how long the replication cycle took. Set the `min part hours` to be comfortably out of reach of the longest replication time.

If the cluster experiences an unusual amount of drive failures, or if you are making ring changes, it might be worthwhile to increase the minimum part hours setting temporarily because replication times will be increasing. If they increase outside of the minimum part hours setting, it increases the chances that you'll have unavailable data. This setting can be dynamically tuned at cluster runtime to optimize the rate at which ring changes can be made.

When you choose a setting, use this in the 'min_part_hours' in the ring builder 'create' command.

Creating the Builder Files

So now we're ready to create the builder files.

The commands we will be running are:

```
swift-ring-builder account.builder create <part_power> <replicas> <min_part_hours>
swift-ring-builder container.builder create <part_power> <replicas> <min_part_hours>
swift-ring-builder object.builder create <part_power> <replicas> <min_part_hours>
```

Now that we understand the values needed for 'part_power', 'replicas' and 'min_part_hours', let's run:

```
$ cd /etc/swift
$ swift-ring-builder account.builder create 18 3 24
$ swift-ring-builder container.builder create 18 3 24
$ swift-ring-builder object.builder create 18 3 24
```

What you should see are three files:

account.builder
container.builder
object.builder

and backup directory, appropriately named *backups*.

And just to take some mystery out of what you have just created let's take a look at it.

```
$ python
Python 2.7.3 (default, Aug  1 2012, 05:14:39)
[GCC 4.6.3] on linux2
Type "help", "copyright", "credits" or "license" for more in-
   formation.
>>> import pickle
>>> print pickle.load(open('object.builder'))
{'_replica2part2dev': None, '_last_part_gather_start': 0,
   'min_part_hours': 24, 'replicas': 3.0, 'parts': 262144,
   'part_power': 18, 'devs': [], 'devs_changed': False, 'ver-
   sion': 0, '_last_part_moves_epoch': None, '_last_part_
   moves': None, '_remove_devs': []}
```

What you're seeing is a Python data structure.

Be sure not to lose these builder files! Never lose the **.builder* files.

For those running SwiftStack, the builder files are automatically backed-up with each change to an off-site location. For on-premise SwiftStack Controller customers, an additional backup target can be specified.

Creating the Rings: Adding Devices

Our next goal is to define how the ring configuration files will be created.

This part of the configuration serves two purposes:

1. It describe the failure boundaries for the cluster by placing each node into a zone.
2. It describe how much data Swift should put on each device in the cluster by giving it a weight

To generate the final 'ring' files, run:

```
$ cd /etc/swift
$ sudo swift-ring-builder account.builder rebalance
```

But at this point the command should complain about dividing by zero. This is because there are not yet any devices in the ring builder files.

Let's go back to the */etc/swift* directory and add devices to the builder files.

Run:

```
$ cd /etc/swift
$ swift-ring-builder account.builder add
```

You should see the help message:

```
$ swift-ring-builder <builder_file> add
z<zone>-<ip>:<port>/<device_name>_<meta> <weight>
```

For each device the commands would look like:

```
$ swift-ring-builder account.builder add z1-10.0.2.15:6000/d1
   100
$ swift-ring-builder container.builder add z1-10.0.2.15:6001/
   d1 100
$ swift-ring-builder object.builder add z1-10.0.2.15:6002/d1
   100
```

...and so on for each device in the cluster.

IP

You need to specify the location of the IP address where each device will be available. This should be a private network that each storage node in the cluster can communicate via rsync and HTTP. It's not necessary that this be layer-2 network.

Port

Each of the account, container, and object servers can run on different ports. By default:

account runs on port 6002

container runs on port 6001

object runs on port 6000

Weight

Each device in the system has a weight. This is a *relative* weight that determines the number of partitions a device (drive) will have. This is a configuration of the ring and it is set as part of the ring building process.

Because this is a relative number it's up to the operator to configure the weights to be used to represent each drive.

For example, when first starting out and each drive is the same size, say 2TB, each drive would receive the weight of '100.0' – think '100%'. Then, when it's time to add capacity and 3TB drives are available, the new 3TB drives would receive the weight of '150.0' being 50% larger.

Another, often simpler, strategy is to use the drive's capacity as a multiplier. For example, the weight of a 2TB drive would be '200.0' and a 3TB drive would be '300.0'.

Note that SwiftStack uses the gigabytes in the drive as a baseline, then dynamically adjusts device weights to manage partition placement when adding/removing devices from the cluster.

Zones

Swift allows zones to be configured to isolate failure boundaries. So if you had a few data centers next to each other, each data center could be a zone. If you had a handful of racks in a data center, then each rack could represent a zone. Typically, deployments create isolated failure boundaries within a datacenter by segmenting the power source and/or network that is serving each zone.

The goal of zones is to allow the cluster to tolerate significant outages of large hunks of storage servers. Do keep in mind that Swift uses "as-unique-as-possible" data placement, which means that zones should only be created for truly fault-tolerant domains.

Building the Rings

The ring files are used to map a request back to a physical location. You must have a running Swift system with builder files created and devices added to the builder file.

Now let's create the ring files. The `rebalance` command creates the actual ring file that is used by the Swift processes.

```
$ cd /etc/swift
$ swift-ring-builder account.builder rebalance
$ swift-ring-builder container.builder rebalance
$ swift-ring-builder object.builder rebalance
```

You should see the following additional files in */etc/swift*:

- account.ring.gz
- container.ring.gz
- object.ring.gz

These files should be copied to each node in the cluster. These ring files are what are copied out to each node in the system. Copy these files to each */etc/swift* directory for each node in the cluster. This is the distilled data structure that tells Swift the data placement of the cluster.

Swift automatically detects new ring data every 15 seconds. When you push out a new ring, you don't have to restart any Swift processes.

Take care that when a node is down that it gets the new ring files when it comes back online. If one node has a different ring file, the node will think that data isn't where it should be and will do its part to move it back to where it's "supposed" to be. For those running SwiftStack, the SwiftStack Controller will ensure that each ring file is correct on each node.

What's happening here is that each device is signing up for its share of the partitions that are out there. During the building process, we decided how many partitions there would be (2^ some number). Now, each device is declaring its relative 'weight' in the system. The rebalancing process, takes all the partitions and assigns them to a device making sure that each device is subscribed according to its weight. That way a device with a weight of 200 gets twice as many partitions as a device with a weight of 100.

The builder files contain all sorts of information about devices in the cluster. In essence, they tell the history of the devices in your Swift cluster. This rebalancing process takes into account how dramatic the changes that were just made are to the cluster. So the builder files keep track of such things as when partitions were last moved around and where partitions are currently. This enables the rebalancer to not move partitions around if they've been moved around recently (sooner than what `min part hours` is set to) and to not reassign partitions to new devices unnecessarily.

Configuring Logging to a Single, Local File

Configure `rsyslog` to create a log location for Swift. In this example, we'll be directing all the log files to a single location.

Create the file */etc/rsyslog.d/0-swift.conf* with contents local0.* /var/log/swift/all.log

```
$ sudo cat 'local0.* /var/log/swift/all.log'
> /etc/rsyslog.d/0-swift.conf
```

make the directory and set permissions:

```
$ sudo mkdir /var/log/swift
$ sudo chown -R syslog.adm /var/log/swift
```

and restart `rsyslog`:

```
$ sudo service rsyslog restart
```

Swift uses `syslog` to help it manage where logs go to. In this example, we sent all the server processes to a single log for 'swift'. In each configuration file is a setting called *log_name*. By default all are set to *swift*.

Logging configuration is automatically configured for SwiftStack deployments. Additionally, external logging and alerting configurations can be configured.

Configuring Proxy Server

The goal of this section is to get the proxy server up and running.

The proxy server:

- Processes incoming HTTP requests
- Looks up locations on the ring
- Interacts with the authentication/authorization middleware
- Forwards on requests to the right account, container, or object server

The first configuration setting for the proxy server is to set the *swift_hash_path_suffix in /etc/swift/swift.conf.*

Hash Path Suffix

The reason for the *swift_hash_path_suffix* is to prevent a potential DOS attack which would result in intermittent PUT failures. If someone knows the hash path suffix, it could be used to know the actual partition where their object would be stored. An attacker could generate containers/objects with the same partition and repeatedly put large files to the same partition until the drive was full.

If the hash prefix is large and unknown, than it's unguessable and someone can't craft a container/object with a known partition. If any one of the disks is full in the Swift cluster, then any request that hits that particular drive will fail because the partition will be full. This could normally be solved by dropping down the weight of that particular drive and shedding a few partitions. However, in an attack situation where the user knows the hash path suffix, a user could deliberately push data to a particular partition.

Edit */etc/swift/swift.conf* and change the *swift_hash_path_suffix* to something secret.

```
$ vi /etc/swift/swift.conf
```

So let's set this to something secret in the */etc/swift/swift.conf*.

```
[swift-hash]
swift_hash_path_suffix = something-secret
```

SwiftStack deployments automatically create a unique 128-bit identifier that is used for the *swift_hash_path_suffix* and ensures that the same *swift_hash_path_suffix* is set cluster-wide.

Let's start up the proxy server process:

```
$ sudo swift-init proxy start
```

You may get an error ending with `KeyError: 'getpwnam(): name not found: swift'`

This means that a user named swift hasn't been created. If you haven't done so, let's do so now.

```
$ sudo useradd swift
```

Setting up TempAuth Authentication & Authorization with Swift

This section covers setting up setting up TempAuth and creating an account on the Swift cluster with TempAuth. TempAuth allows you to specify accounts in configuration files.

For this configuration, you'll need to:

- Start up the Swift proxy service which can create accounts
- Start the Swift account service so that those accounts can be created
- Install memcache so that authentication tokens can persist

How Swift authentication works is that you connect to an authentication service and it gives you a token. Then you take that token to the Swift API service and that token is used to authorize that request.

The way that the authentication process happens is as follows.

A request is made to an authentication service. The client sends `X-Auth-User` and `X-Auth-Key` in the HTTP header. The server responds with either a response code of `200` (meaning that the request was authenticated) and a token in the HTTP response header called `X-Auth-Token`.

The client takes that token and uses it for subsequent requests to make API requets to upload, download, create containers, etc. The API service validates that token to make sure that it is valid. If the token is ever rejected by the API service, the client simply makes another request to the authentication API to obtain another token.

For TempAuth with Swift, the auth server creates tokens, sends the token back in the HTTP request and stores the token in memcache. When API requests are made the API service looks up the token in memcache to see if it is valid.

If you look at */etc/swift/proxy-server.conf*, you can find the section that describes tempauth:

```
[filter:tempauth]
use = egg:swift#tempauth
# You can override the default log routing for this filter
   here:
...
# <account> is from the user_<account>_<user> name.
# Here are example entries, required for running the tests:
user_admin_admin = admin .admin .reseller_admin
user_test_tester = testing .admin
user_test2_tester2 = testing2 .admin
user_test_tester3 = testing3
```

With tempauth, users are defined in the configuration file itself with the format:

```
user_<account>_<user> = <key> [group] [group] [...] [stor-
    age_url]
```

See the SwiftStack blog for more details on TempAuth configuration (*http://swiftstack.com/blog/2012/01/04/swift-tempauth/*).

You can create an account of your own:

```
user_myaccount_me = secretpassword .admin .reseller_admin
```

Also set:

```
allow_account_management = true
```

Now start up the account service, and because we have changed the proxy server configuration, restart the proxy server.

```
$ sudo swift-init account start
$ sudo swift-init proxy restart
```

Keep in mind that TempAuth is appropriately named *Temp*Auth. Proxy server processes must be restarted when adding/removing accounts and credentials are stored in plaintext.

SwiftStack clusters can be configured with additional authentication integrations with the SwiftStack Controller. Here are additional authentication options available with SwiftStack:

SwiftStack Auth: A fast flat-file is deployed on each node with hashed passwords. Does not require a proxy restart. Users can be added via Controller web-interface. REST API to programmatically add/remove users. Great for application development, where there are a relatively fixed number of accounts on the clusters.

Keystone Auth: Enable Keystone to integrate with an OpenStack compute deployment.

Active Directory: Enable Active Directory for the cluster to participate in the AD domain.

LDAP: Enable LDAP authentication, for integration with an OpenLDAP service.

SWAuth: Uses the Swift cluster itself to store account data.

CSAuth: Enables integration with CloudStack.

Now let's create the account in Swift.

```
$ curl -v -H 'X-Auth-User: myaccount:me' -H 'X-Auth-Key:
    secretpassword' http://localhost/auth/v1.0/
* About to connect() to localhost port 80 (#0)
*   Trying ::1... Connection refused
*   Trying 127.0.0.1... connected
* Connected to localhost (127.0.0.1) port 80 (#0)
> GET /auth/v1.0/ HTTP/1.1
> User-Agent: curl/7.19.7 (i486-pc-linux-gnu) libcurl/7.19.7
   OpenSSL/0.9.8k zlib/1.2.3.3 libidn/1.15
> Host: localhost:80
> Accept: */*
> X-Auth-User: myaccount:me
> X-Auth-Key: secretpassword
>
< HTTP/1.1 200 OK
< X-Storage-Url: http://127.0.0.1:80/v1/AUTH_myaccount
< X-Storage-Token: AUTH_tk265318ae5e7e46f1890a441c08b5247f
< X-Auth-Token: AUTH_tk265318ae5e7e46f1890a441c08b5247f
< X-Trans-Id: txc75adf112791425e82826d6e3989be4d
< Content-Length: 0
< Date: Tue, 21 Mar 2013 22:48:40 GMT
<
```

See the `X-Auth-Token` in the HTTP response? TempAuth stores them in memcache so that future API requests can authenticate a token.

Be sure to install and start memcache if it's not already installed.

```
$ sudo apt-get install memcached
```

This should install and start memcahce.

Let's take a look at its entry in memcache.

```
$ python
>>> import swift.common.memcached as memcached
>>> memcache = memcached.MemcacheRing(['127.0.0.1:11211'])
>>> print memcache.get('AUTH_/user/myaccount:me')
AUTH_tk58ad6d3ca1754ca78405828d72e37458
>>> print memcache.get('AUTH_/token/AUTH_tk58ad6d3ca-
   1754ca78405828d72e37458')
(1308804765.9103661, 'myaccount,myaccount:me')
ctl-d
```

Now you're ready to make your first request. List the containers in your account.

```
$ curl -v -H 'X-Storage-Token: AUTH_tk58ad6d3ca-
   1754ca78405828d72e37458' http://127.0.0.1/v1/AUTH_myac-
   count/
* About to connect() to 127.0.0.1 port 80 (#0)
*   Trying 127.0.0.1... connected
* Connected to 127.0.0.1 (127.0.0.1) port 80 (#0)
> GET /v1/AUTH_admin HTTP/1.1
> User-Agent: curl/7.19.7 (i486-pc-linux-gnu) libcurl/7.19.7
   OpenSSL/0.9.8k zlib/1.2.3.3 libidn/1.15
> Host: 127.0.0.1:80
> Accept: */*
> X-Storage-Token: AUTH_tk215c5706a61048c09819cd6ba60142ef
>
< HTTP/1.1 204 No Content
< X-Account-Object-Count: 0
< X-Account-Bytes-Used: 0
< X-Account-Container-Count: 0
< Accept-Ranges: bytes
< X-Trans-Id: txafe3c83ed76e46d2a9536dd61d9fcf09
< Content-Length: 0
< Date: Tue, 21 Jun 2011 23:23:23 GMT
<
```

Congratulations you've just created an account in Swift.

Starting the Container Service

Accounts and containers are just sqlite databases. For each account, there is an account database that contains a listing of all the containers. For each container, there is a container database that stores all of the objects for those containers. Each of these databases is stored in the cluster and replicated in the same manner as the objects – wholly, in triplicate.

```
$ sudo swift-init container start
```

Using the token from before, run:

```
$ curl -v -H 'X-Storage-Token: AUTH_tk58ad6d3ca-
   1754ca78405828d72e37458' -X PUT http://127.0.0.1/v1/AUTH_
   myaccount/contain_this
```

201 Created

Success!

What is happening:

- The proxy server will make a request to the account server to update the account database of a new container.
- The proxy server makes a request to the container server to create the container database record.

We can take a look at the list of files in the data directories to see the container databases that have been created. We can open that database up to view the account and container database and examine its contents.

For examples, an account database would be located at a location like: */srv/node/d2/account/497/e15/7c7d7a8558f1774e7f06d95094136e15/7c7d7a8558f1774e7f-06d95094136e15.db*

What's interesting here is that these account/container databases are just sqlite databases. Let's take a look at one of them.

install sqlite3

```
$ sudo apt-get install sqlite3
```

copy and paste the path to one of those account databases and open it with the command:

```
$ sqlite3 /srv/node/d2/accounts/497/e15/7c7d7a8558f1774e7f-
    06d95094136e15/7c7d7a8558f1774e7f06d95094136e15.db

sqlite> .tables
account_stat    container    incoming_sync    outgoing_sync
sqlite> select * from account_stat;
AUTH_admin|1308715316.66344|1308715316.64684|0|0|0|0|
    00000000000000000000000000000000|ccfa951a-82a5-42fc-96c1-
    7c3e116e6e2e||0|
sqlite> .quit
```

Starting the Object Server

Now let's start the object server processes. The object server is the service that stores the objects themselves.

```
$ sudo swift-init object start
```

Now you can use the swift command-line client (covered in Chapter 3) to upload a file.

```
$ swift -A http://127.0.0.1/auth/v1.0/ -U myaccount:me -K
    secretpassword upload conatin_this some_file
```

When a client makes a REST API request to PUT an object into an existing container, the request is received by the cluster. The first thing that happens is for the cluster to figure out where the heck this data is going to go. To do this, the account name, container name, and object name are all used to determine which partition this thing should live in.

Then a lookup in the ring figures out which storage nodes contain the partitions in question.

The data then is sent to each storage node where it is placed in the appropriate partition. However, a quorum is required! At least two of the three writes must be successful before the client is notified that the upload was successful.

Next the container database is updated to reflect that there is a new object in it.

When we made the download request, the request comes in for an account/container/object. Using the same consistent hashing, the partition name is generated. A lookup in the ring reveals which storage nodes contain that partition. A request is made to one of the storage nodes to fetch the object and if that fails, requests are made to the other nodes.

Running the Replicators, Auditors and Consistency processes

The replicators run to copy back missing data. The auditors check for missing data.

This section will cover:

- Configuring `rsyncd.conf`
- Starting the replicator processes

First, let's install and configure `rsync`

```
$ sudo apt-get install rsync
```

edit /etc/default/rsync

```
$ vi /etc/default/rsync
```

set

RSYNC_ENABLE=true

Create /etc/rsyncd.conf:

```
$ vi /etc/rsyncd.conf
uid = swift
gid = swift
log file = /var/log/rsyncd.log
pid file = /var/run/rsyncd.pid

[account]
max connections = 25
path = /srv/node/
read only = false
lock file = /var/lock/account.lock

[container]
max connections = 25
path = /srv/node/
read only = false
lock file = /var/lock/container.lock

[object]
max connections = 25
path = /srv/node/
read only = false
lock file = /var/lock/object.lock

$ service rsync start
```

Now you should test that `rsync` is running with these debugging commands.

```
$ rsync localhost::
$ rsync localhost::account
$ rsync localhost::container
$ rsync localhost::object
```

Note that with SwiftStack nodes, `rsync` is automatically configured.

```
$ sudo swift-init account-replicator start
$ sudo swift-init container-replicator start
$ sudo swift-init object-replicator start
```

In order to ensure that there are three copies of the data, replicators examine each partition. Each partition calls out to the other, replicated partitions on the other devices to see if there are any changes.

How does it know if replication needs to take place? It does this by examining hashes. A hash file is created for each partition which contains hashes of each directory in the partition. The three hash files are compared. If all the hashes are the same, then no replication takes place. If the hashes are different, then it's time to replicate and the directory that needs to be replicated is copied over.

This is where the partitions come in handy, with fewer "things" in the system, larger chunks of data are transferred around (vs. lots of little TCP connections, which is inefficient) and there is a consistent number of hashes to compare.

The newest partition wins.

It's very important to configure NTP (Network Time Protocol) to ensure that each node has the same sense of time. SwiftStack Controller will ensure that each SwiftStack node in the cluster has consistent time configured.

Next, start up the remaining processes.

While we have been starting the Swift processes individually, the **swift-init** command has an 'all' command to start up all the Swift processes.

Run:

```
$ sudo swift-init all start
```

This will start up the auditors which will inspect data on disk for intermittent failures. It will also start up the updaters which will roll-up point-in-time account and container information. Finally, an account 'reaper' will be started which will cleanup deleted accounts.

The full list of Swift processes that should be running is the following:

swift-account-server
swift-account-replicator
swift-account-auditor
swift-account-reaper

swift-container-server
swift-container-replicator
swift-container-updater
swift-container-auditor

swift-object-server
swift-object-replicator
swift-object-updater
swift-object-auditor
swift-proxy-server

No Pain, No Gain

This concludes this section on installing OpenStack Swift. We went through the 'manual' process as it serves as a good jumping off point for what needs to be automated for a production deployment. With an understanding of what is happening 'under the hood', you can be a more informed operator of the tools that you will use to deploy and manage your cluster.

Part II

Installing OpenStack Swift with SwiftStack

The next part of this chapter provides step-by-step instructions on how to install and configure the SwiftStack node software with OpenStack Swift. We will install a single node, but additional nodes can be installed in the same fashion.

SwiftStack is a Software Defined Storage (SDS) system. One aspect of an SDS system, is that the management and configuration are decoupled from the storage. In this example we will use the SwiftStack Controller Service. This is a decoupled storage controller that is provided as a service over the Internet. However, an on-premise SwiftStack Controller is also available so that the SDS controller can be on site.

Creating a SwiftStack Controller Service Account

To get started with SwiftStack, first go signup for a Controller Service account at: *http://swiftstack.com/signup/*.

Figure 4.1

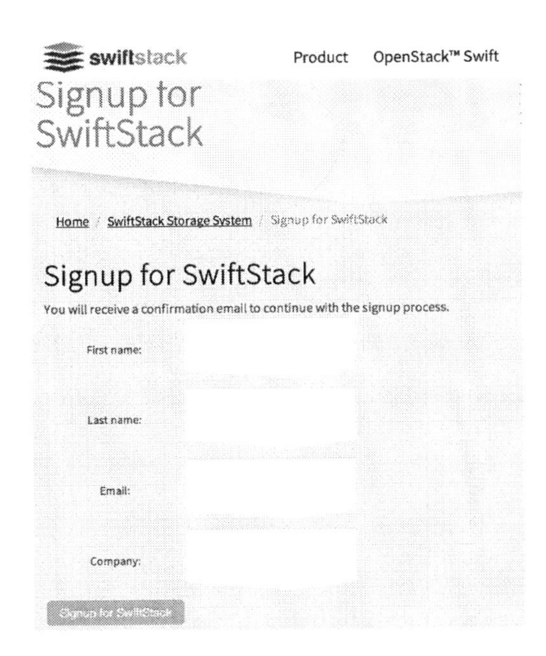

Once you complete the signup process and create the necessary accounts you can continue with the installation process.

Installing SwiftStack Node Software

SwiftStack supports Ubuntu 12.04 LTS Precise Server (64-bit) and CentOS/Red-Hat 6.3 Server (64-bit), which is the only software that needs to be installed before installing SwiftStack. The nodes you install SwiftStack on will need to be able to access the Internet to reach the SwiftStack Controller, which is where you will configure, manage, and monitor your cluster. (An on-premise SwiftStack Controller is also available.) All commands on the nodes will also need to be performed with root privileges.

Ubuntu

To install the SwiftStack Nodes software on Ubuntu, run the following command as root:

```
# curl https://platform.swiftstack.com/install_ubuntu
```

CentOS / Red Hat

To install the SwiftStack Nodes software on CentOS or RedHat, run the following command:

```
# curl https://platform.swiftstack.com/install_centos
```

Executing this command will allow you to output the commands that will be run to install the SwiftStack node software. Note that if you have previously installed OpenStack Swift on the node, it will be replaced with the version included in the SwiftStack node software. When you are ready, go ahead and run the command:

For Ubuntu:

```
# curl https://platform.swiftstack.com/install_ubuntu | bash
```

For CentOS / Red Hat

```
# curl https://platform.swiftstack.com/install_centos | bash
```

Claiming a New Node

After the SwiftStack Nodes software has been installed, the node registers itself with the SwiftStack Controller and obtains a URL used to 'claim' the node. The claim URL will be displayed in the terminal as soon as the installation completes.

```
+--------------------------------------------------------------------+
| Please claim this node to continue the installation process.       |
|                                                                    |
| Your claim URL is:                                                 |
| https://platform.swiftstack.com/claim/3e873021-8da3-11e2-          |
|       9108-000c29f59d79                                            |
+--------------------------------------------------------------------+
```

The above example is for the SwiftStack Controller Service. If you are using an on-premise SwiftStack Controller, then the node would be installing from a private Controller. The claim URL would also be for that on-premise SwiftStack Controller.

To continue installation, follow the claim URL with a browser and click `Claim`. The SwiftStack node will open a secure VPN connection between itself and the SwiftStack Controller.

The node will need to be able to communicate out over the following ports to the SwiftStack Controller:

443 / HTTPS - Initial claim process & configuration

1194 / VPN (UDP) - Communications channel

At no point does the controller have any access to data that is stored on a SwiftStack Node.

Creating a Cluster

Create a new cluster giving it a name and specifying its front-facing IP address. This is the IP address that clients would use to access the cluster. If it's configured with your DNS, you can optionally specify a hostname to use.

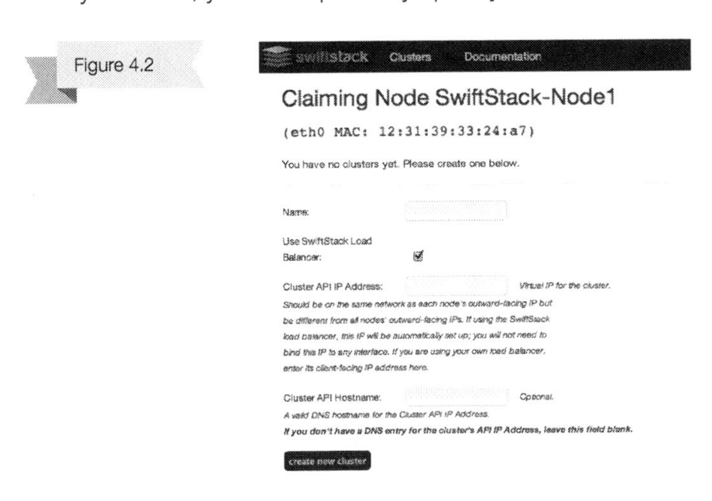

Figure 4.2

Provisioning a Swiftstack Node

On the cluster configuration page click the `Provision` button for the node that is to be provisioned. The nodes that haven't been provisioned appear highlighted in yellow.

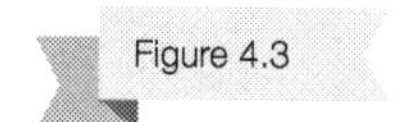
Figure 4.3

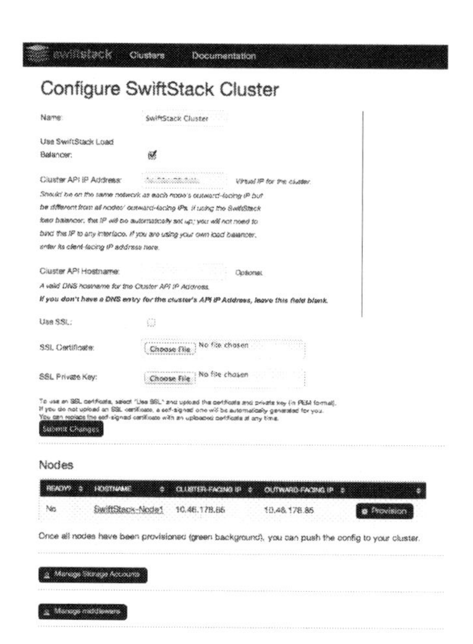

Next, perform two steps. First, format the devices and then `Add` the devices.

Click `Format`, then `Change`. This will take a few minutes as the drives format.

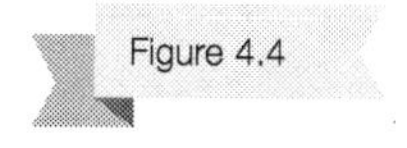
Figure 4.4

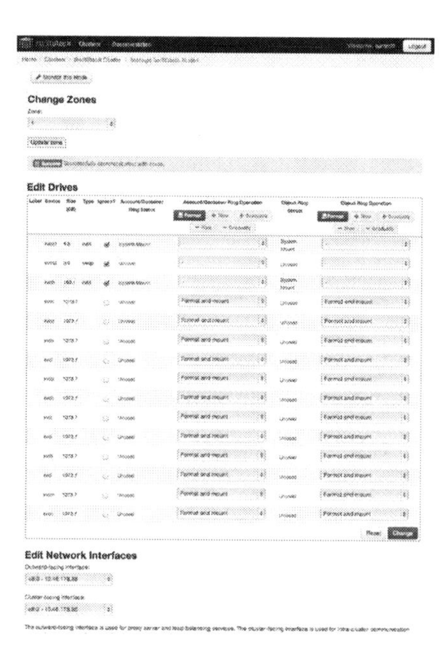

Next, click `+Now` for both `Account/Container Ring Operation` and `Object Ring Operation`.

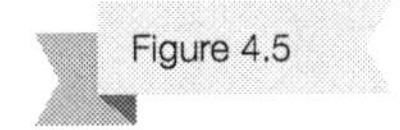
Figure 4.5

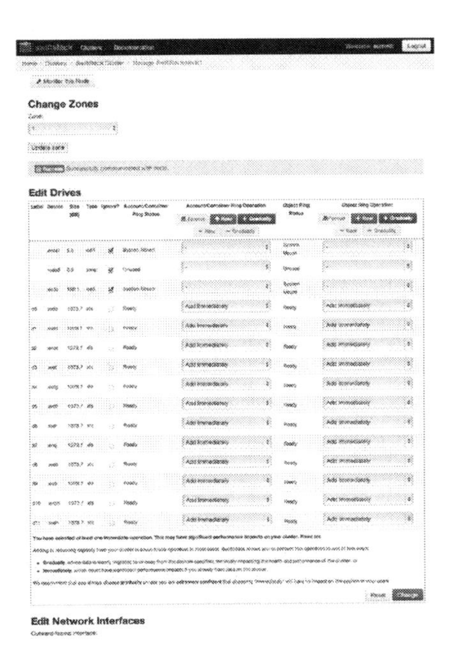

Note that for large, multi-node deployments, there are scripts available to automate the provisioning of large numbers of nodes.

Finally, click the `Enable Node`. Now the node is ready to participate in the cluster.

Any drive can be assigned to storing account/container data, but Swiftstack generally recommends using faster media, such as SSDs. The drive roles can be configured on this page.

Adding Users

The next step is to add a user account. To configure an account, click `Manage Storage Accounts`.

Add an account with the desired username and password.

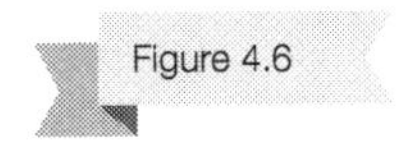
Figure 4.6

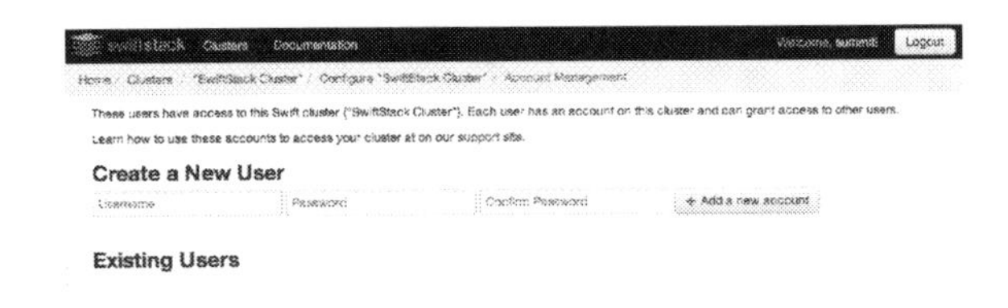

The authentication system built into SwiftStack is a fast, flat-file that is deployed on each node with hashed passwords. While it does require a configuration push out to the cluster, it does not require a proxy restart. Users can be added via Controller web interface or via a REST API to programmatically add/remove users. This is recommended for application development, where there are a relatively fixed number of accounts on the clusters.

Note that SwiftStack clusters can be configured with additional authentication integrations with the SwiftStack Controller. Please contact (*support@swiftstack.com*) to enable other options. Additional authentication options are available with SwiftStack:

> **Keystone Auth:** Enable Keystone to integrate with an OpenStack compute deployment.
>
> **Active Directory:** Enable Active Directory for the cluster to participate in the AD domain.
>
> **LDAP:** Enable LDAP authentication, for integration with an OpenLDAP service.
>
> **SWAuth:** Uses the Swift cluster itself to store account data.

Enabling Swift Web Console

Next, enable desired middleware, including a user web console. Click on the `Manage Middleware` button to configure.

Enable `Static Web`, `TempUrl`, `FormPost`, `Name Check` and `Swift Web Console`

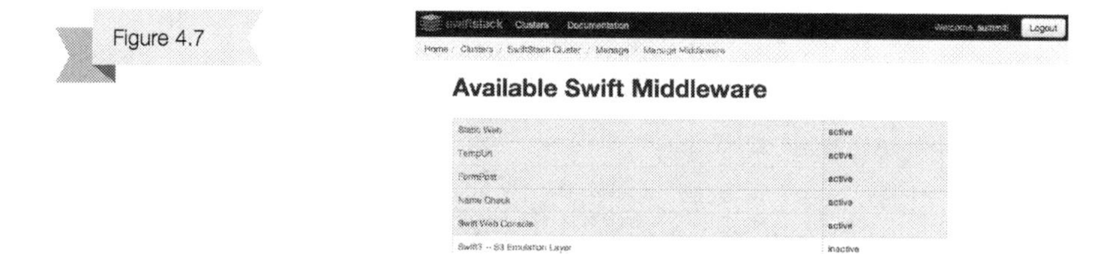

Figure 4.7

Push Config

Finally, push the configuration to the cluster.

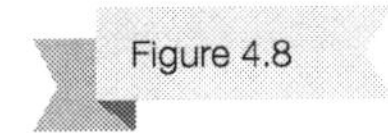
Figure 4.8

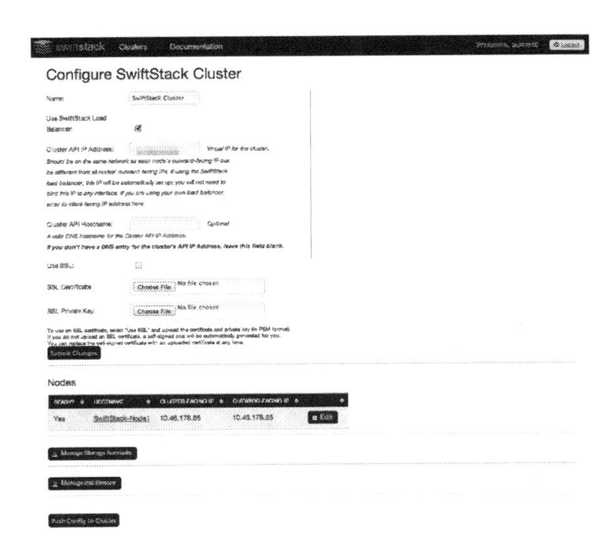

Pushing Config to the cluster performs the following actions:

- Adds appropriate devices and nodes into the Swift builder file.
- Creates a Swift ring.
- Adds any additional user accounts that had been created or modified.
- Creates new swift configurations based on, network settings and the settings available in `Tune Cluster`.
- Notifies each node in the cluster that new configuration settings are available and should be downloaded.
- Pulls the new configuration files and restarts processes (when necessary) for each node in the cluster.

While the configuration is being pushed, the following status message is displayed:

Figure 4.9

When the configuration push is done, your SwiftStack cluster will be available at the IP specified in the Cluster API IP address. Do note, that it takes about 5-10 minutes for the SwiftStack Controller to rebuild the ring and push the new configuration out to the cluster.

Uploading via Web Console

SwiftStack makes uploading easy through a built-in web console to upload/download and manage data. After the configuration push is completed, click the `Web Console` link.

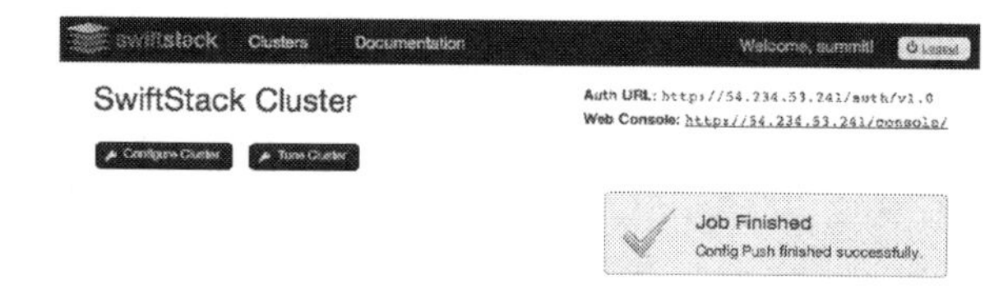

Sign in with the storage account and password created.

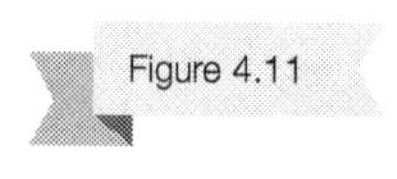

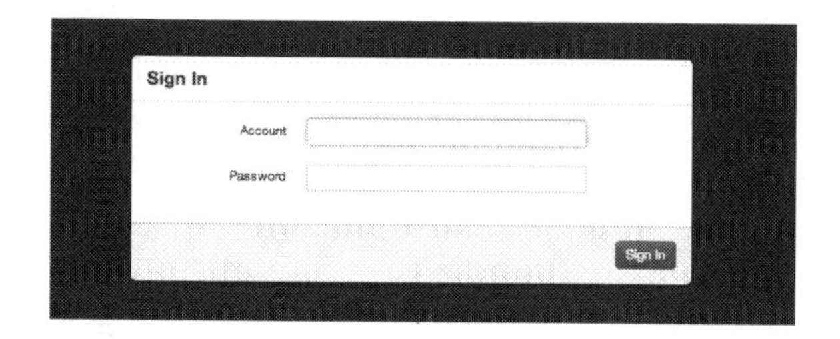

Create a container:

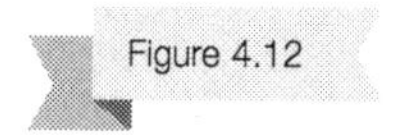

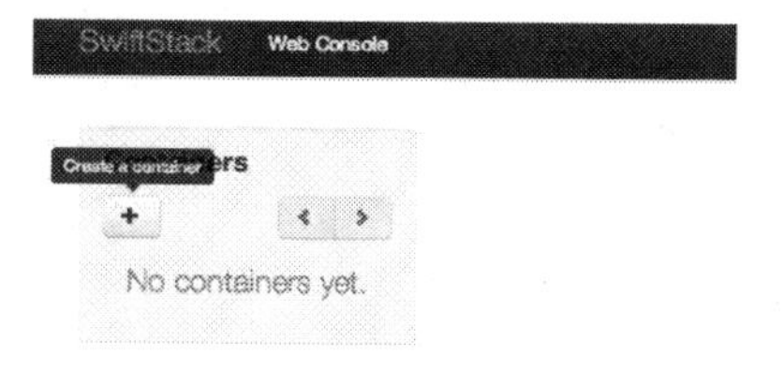

Upload files!

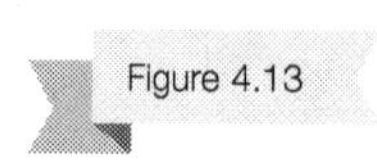

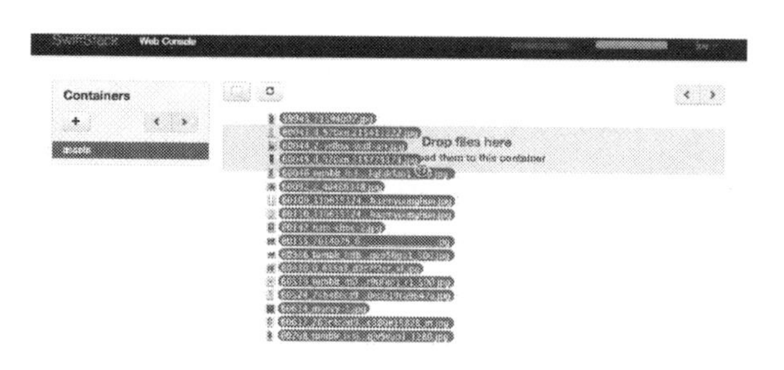

Using the Swift API

Of course, all the same Swift API commands can be used as detailed in Chapter 3.

Conclusion

Congratulations! Installation is half the battle and if you have gotten this far, you likely have your very own Swift cluster up and running. Going through the installation 'long hand,' should have given you some perspective and understanding of the details. Then, by walking through the SwiftStack install you saw an example workflow of how it can be automated.

We have seen a number of options during installation, however we have more to go. There is much to configure when starting up a Swift cluster. Coming up in the next chapters is more information about the Swift Controller, building a Swift cluster, how to fine-tune a Swift cluster, as well as what to do *when*, not *if*, hardware fails.

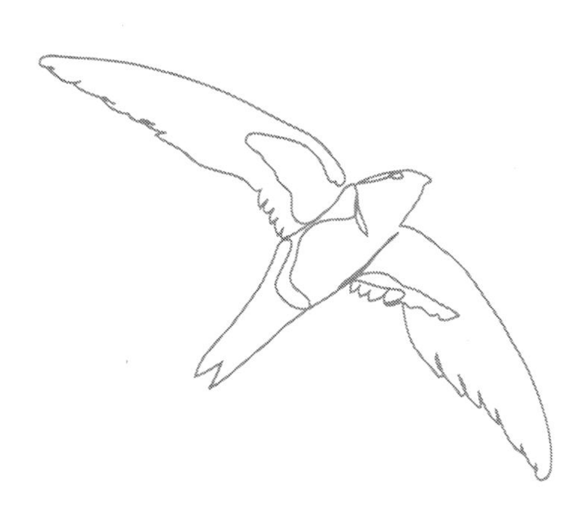

CHAPTER FIVE

Software Defined Storage with the SwiftStack Controller

In the previous chapter you learned how to install a run-time stack with Swift using the SwiftStack Nodes software and the SwiftStack Controller. In this chapter, you will learn how a Software Defined Storage (SDS) system works.

Software Defined Storage

A Software Defined Storage (SDS) system separates the intelligence and access from the underlying physical hardware.

There are four critical components to build an SDS system.

- Routing & Services
- Storage Intelligence
- Physical Hardware
- Controller

Figure 5.1 ***Components of Software Defined Storage***

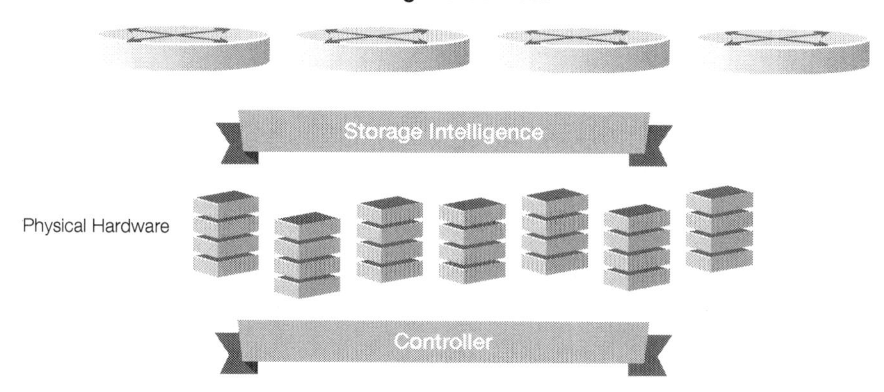

Routing & Services

The routing and services tier acts as a gateway to the storage system. Pools of routing and services can be distributed across multiple data centers and geographies. The routing and services layer scales out with each additional node allowing for more capacity for data access.

The router in an SDS system can route storage requests around hardware and networking faults. When there is a hardware failure, the router applies simple rules to service the request by assembling necessary data chunks or retrieving replicas from non-failed locations.

The services in an SDS system account for access control, enable supported protocols, and respond to API requests.

Storage Intelligence

In an SDS system, reliability is the responsibility of the software, not the hardware. Replication and data integrity tactics are used to ensure that data does not become corrupt and that lost data is recovered.

Physical Hardware

The physical hardware stores the bits on disk with an SDS system. Each storage node is not responsible for ensuring durability of its own data, as that is the responsibility of the storage intelligence.

Controller

An SDS system must have a decoupled control plane to manage the other components in the system. Because each other component is a member of a distributed system, a controller is required to manage the system as a whole.

A controller will dynamically tune the system to optimize performance. A controller will allow for faster recoveries when hardware fails and allow an operator to respond to operational events. A crucial function of an SDS system is to orchestrate capacity – storage, networking, routing & services – for the entire cluster.

Benefits of Software Defined Storage

It is key for an SDS system to be able to effectively manage scale and drive operational efficiencies in the infrastructure. Capacity management is a lot simpler with an SDS system, because each component is a member of a distributed system. Because of this upgrades, expansions, and decommissions can be achieved without any downtime and with no need for 'forklift' data migration.

There is no application sharding or managing volumes which can drive operational knowledge and complexity into applications because the SDS system is one cohesive system. Users do not need to ask for or know 'which storage pool' should be used because there is only one namespace.

The separation of physical hardware from the software allows for mix and match hardware configurations within the same storage system. Drives of varying capacity, or even CPU capability can be used in the same system. The benefit is that capacity increments can be more incremental. This allows for just-in-time purchasing and lets you take advantage of the technology innovation curve.

SwiftStack: Software Defined Storage for Object Storage

For the remainder of the chapter, we will cover in detail SwiftStack's take on an SDS. We will cover the features and capacities of the SwiftStack Controller.

SwiftStack Node Software

In SDS-speak, the SwiftStack Node software enables physical hardware to provide router and services functionality, provide the storage intelligence, or service both functions.

The SwiftStack Node software includes the latest, stable version of Swift, several other components required to run Swift in production, and a package-based installer which installs the entire run-time stack on the server. The physical hardware can be provided by multiple vendors and built with standard, off-the-shelf components. The SwiftStack Node software can currently be installed on Ubuntu 12.04 LTS Precise Server (64-bit) or CentOS/Red Hat 6.3 Server (64-bit), the operating system is the only software that needs to be installed before installing SwiftStack.

The following components are included with the SwiftStack Node software:

For routing and services:

- Swift proxy server
- Authentication services
- Built-in load balancer
- SSL termination for HTTPS services
- Web client / user portal
- Usage stats collection agents

For storage:

- Storage services
- All storage intelligence services (auditing, replication, consistency checks)
- Monitoring agents
    - System monitoring stats collection
    - Disk management tools
- Storage stats collection agents

The nodes will need access to SwiftStack Controller, which is where you will configure, manage, and monitor your cluster.

Once the SwiftStack Node software is installed on a server, it contacts the SwiftStack Controller via https (port 443) to register itself. When this process is successful, the node will obtain an identification from a SwiftStack Controller. A 'claim' URL will then be created so that the operator can continue the install process. Once the operator goes to that URL, the SwiftStack node will open a secure VPN connection to the controller over UDP (port 1194), where only outgoing connections are allowed over the secure VPN connection and all incoming connections are blocked.

Figure 5.2 ***SwiftStack Controller & SwiftStack Nodes***

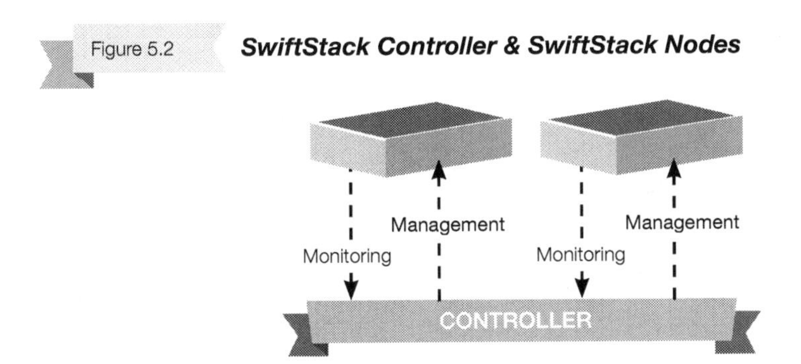

It is via this VPN connection that the Controller manages the node(s) and receives monitoring data that is stored and reported in the Controller. To understand how that process works, let's proceed to the SwiftStack Controller.

SwiftStack Controller

Figure 5.3 ***The SwiftStack Controller***

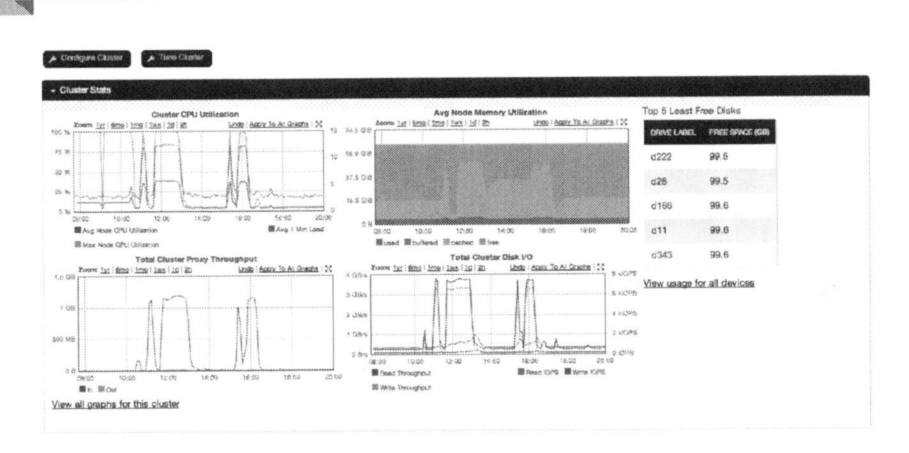

A key characteristic of the SwiftStack SDS system is that management and configuration of the storage nodes are decoupled from the physical hardware. While the actual storage services are run on the servers where the SwiftStack Node software is installed, the management, control, and monitoring is conducted off-band via a decoupled storage controller. This approach has many benefits as operators can now choose how their storage is scaled and managed and how users can store and access data - all driven programmatically for the entire storage tier, independent of where the storage resources are deployed.

To understand how the SwiftStack Controller works, let's review some of the key features.

Management of Nodes

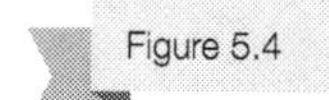

Figure 5.4 ***SwiftStack Node Management***

Once the node has established a connection with the Controller via the VPN connection, the operator can now manage the node via the Controller. The management of nodes through the Controller is secured. Only outgoing connections from the node are allowed to establish the VPN connection to the controller. No inbound connections are used for management. In addition, the node can only accept a limited number of commands that originate from the controller, specifically:

- Pushing new configuration files
- Activating new configurations
- Querying devices for drive discovery/inventory synchronization
- Formatting devices
- Unmounting devices
- Querying for network interfaces
- Querying for general system information (RAM / hostname / CPU core count)

Deployment Automation

Figure 5.5 ***SwiftStack Cluster Management***

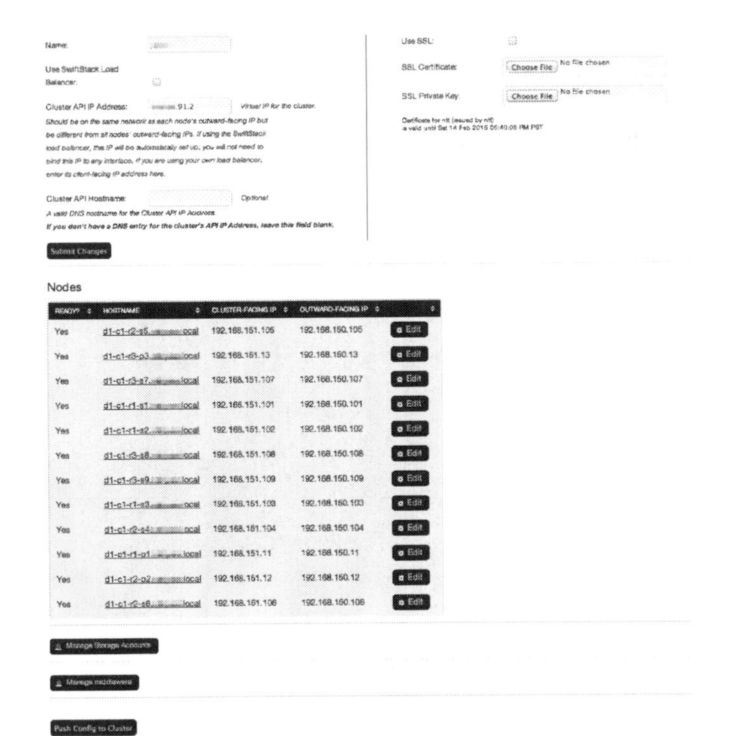

In the Controller UI, the operator can configure individual nodes and configure them into clusters. Once the controller has established 'control' over a specific node, the operator will be able to trigger several different setup and deployment tasks via the Controller UI, including:

- Configuring networking interfaces
- Configuring nodes and formatting drives
- Deploying account, container, and object rings
- Configuring availability zones based on hardware topology

For large scale clusters, this process can also be handled via command line and scripted for automation. The process of deploying the SwiftStack Node software can also be integrated with configuration management tools, such as Chef and Puppet.

Centralized Management

The SwiftStack Controller is inherently multi-tenant. This means that in the same controller, you can configure and manage storage, which can be located in geographically distant locations. By centralizing the control and management, you will ensure that they are consistently deployed, managed, and monitored. This drives operational efficiencies in the infrastructure which will let you do more with fewer resources.

Figure 5.6 ***Centralized Management through the SwiftStack Controller***

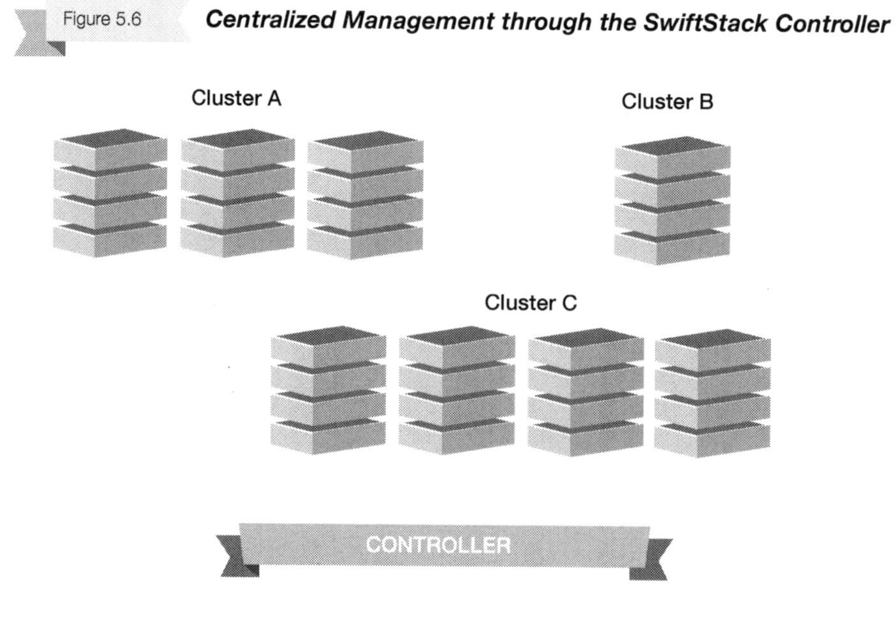

Capacity Management

The SwiftStack Controller also orchestrates capacity additions and removals. When it is time to add storage capacity, it can be done safely without service interruption. Likewise, when a failing drive is identified or when decommissioning a node, data can be slowly migrated off of the device.

Key capacity management features include the ability to:

- Safely add additional capacity on a live cluster
- Gradually remove failing drives
- Gradually decommission storage nodes
- Monitor cluster capacity

Node and Cluster Monitoring

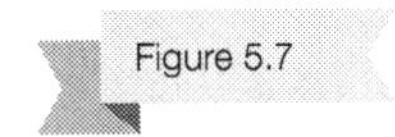

Figure 5.7 ***SwiftStack Node Monitoring***

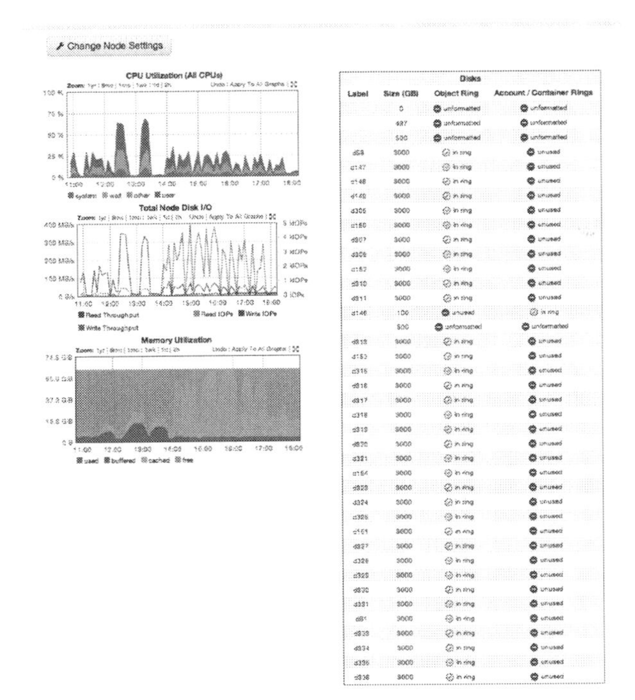

The SwiftStack Controller also provide metrics you need to make informed decisions about how to manage and scale your cluster. A SwiftStack node is instrumented at every layer to provide diagnostics, monitoring data, and alerts to the Controller, which significantly shortens the time to resolve potential bottlenecks and hardware failures. The Controller also provides integrated monitoring specifically designed for OpenStack Swift. Over 500 data points are collected about each node. By visualizing these data points, the Controller enables operators to quickly diagnose issues and potential bottlenecks in the cluster.

Key monitoring features include:

- Visibility into every part of the storage system
- Extensive graphs of monitoring data
- The ability to quickly select time-range and apply across all graphs
- Alerts dashboard

SwiftStack monitoring can also be integrated with Ganglia, Nagios, and other monitoring tools.

On-Premise or As-a-Service

Since the SwiftStack Controller is decoupled from the actual storage nodes, it can be deployed in your datacenter or accessed as-a-service via the SwiftStack Controller Service available at *http://swiftstack.com*. Since the controller is multi-tenant, it supports a hierarchy of organizations (or customers), accounts within those organizations, and clusters within those accounts.

Conclusion

Now that you've learned about the features and capacities of the SwiftStack Controller, you're ready to move on and learn how to set up (Chapter 6) and operate (Chapter 7) your cluster(s).

CHAPTER SIX

Setting Up a Swift Cluster

In this chapter you'll learn how to plan, configure, and set up a Swift cluster. You'll also see some examples of globally distributed clusters.

Planning a Swift Deployment

As we learned in the previous chapters, Swift is designed to store and retrieve whole files via HTTP across a cluster of industry-standard servers and drives, using replication to ensure data reliability and fault tolerance. While this model enables you to take advantage of commodity hardware, it requires upfront planning, validation, and testing to ensure that you select a suitable hardware configuration for your intended workload.

SwiftStack works with several vendors who provide hardware solutions for OpenStack Swift. This ranges from qualified chassis from major OEM partners to pre-integrated racks from recommended VARs.

When selecting hardware for your Swift cluster, it is important to determine which configuration provides the best balance of I/O performance, capacity, and cost for your workload. For instance, customer-facing web applications with a large number of concurrent users will have a different profile than one that is used primarily for archiving.

In most clusters, there are two roles: proxy nodes and storage nodes. The SwiftStack package-based installer contains both proxy server components and storage server components, which can either be run on the same physical node for smaller clusters or be split out in separate tiers for larger deployments. For larger-scale and high-performance clusters, the account and container metadata tier can also be split out into a separate hardware layer, leveraging high-performance media, such as SSDs, for fast metadata storage and retrieval.

When planning a Swift deployment, a fair bit of attention also needs to be paid to how the networking is set up and configured. While all networking in a Swift cluster is done via Layer-3, a Swift cluster will have several different network segments.

- First is a front-facing network for API access. If an external load balancer is used you'll need to consider how you will accomodate this.
- Second, a storage network serving the proxy nodes' communication to the storage nodes and communication between the storage nodes.
- A route to a SwiftStack Controller. For an on-premise SwiftStack Controller, this would be an internal route. For the SwiftStack Controller Service, this would be a route to *platform.swiftstack.com*.
- A management network for IPMI, iLO, etc. used for hardware management.

This chapter will guide you through the hardware selection process and network configuration options.

The Proxy Tier

Proxy nodes handle all incoming API requests. Once a proxy server receives a request, it will determine which storage node to connect to based on the URL of the object. When a client uploads data to SwiftStack, the proxy tier will write data as uniquely as possible in the storage tier. A quorum is required — at least two of the three writes must be successful before the client is notified that the upload was successful.

Proxy services also coordinate responses, handle failures, and coordinate timestamps. As the proxy tier uses a shared-nothing architecture, it can be scaled as needed based on projected workloads. If separated into its own tier, a minimum of two nodes should be deployed in the proxy tier for redundancy. Should one proxy node fail, the other(s) will take over.

Having the proxy services in their own tier enables read/write access to be scaled out independently of storage capacity. For example, if the cluster has high demand for data access, many proxy nodes can be provisioned. However, if the cluster is being used primarily for archival purposes, fewer proxy nodes are needed.

SwiftStack Load Balancing

SwiftStack is configured with a built-in load balancer which is enabled when `Use SwiftStack Load Balancer` is checked.

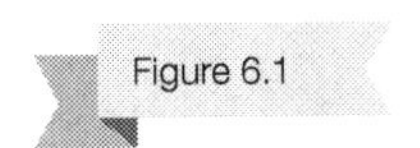
Figure 6.1

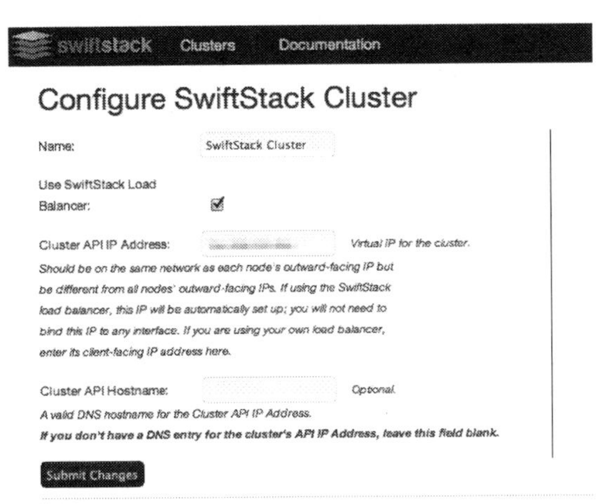

Each node that is serving the proxy will share a Virtual IP and must be on the same layer-2 network as the other proxy nodes. Each proxy node is listening for who is taking load-balancing responsibilities and if one of the proxy nodes goes down, another will take responsibility.

External Load Balancing

An external load balancer is used when the load balancing capacity exceeds the capability of a single node and can be configured by using a health check URL for each proxy node.

Further details on load balancer configuration follow the examples later in this chapter.

SSL Termination

The proxy tier also includes SSL termination. For most deployments, SSL will be used to encrypt traffic between the client and the SwiftStack cluster. As SSL adds processing load to establish sessions between clients, more capacity in the access layer will need to be provisioned.

With SwiftStack, this can be enabled on the cluster configuration page.

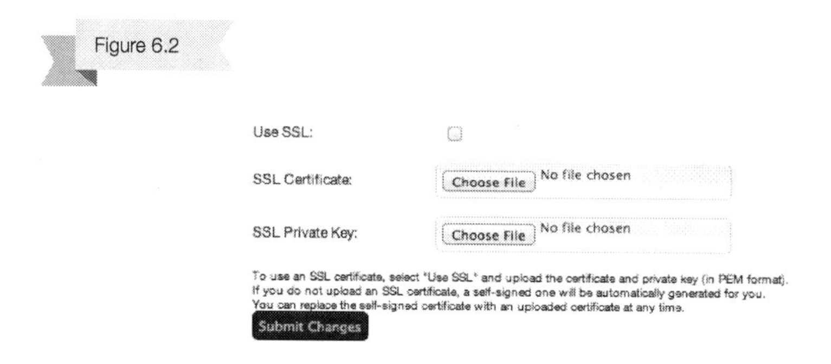

Figure 6.2

The SwiftStack Controller validates that certificate and key match and will apply the certificate across each node in the cluster which makes certificate deployment less error prone. For convenience, a self-signed SSL certificate will be auto-created for lab/test environments if the box is checked and no SSL certificate is uploaded.

Authentication Services

In addition to load balancing and SSL termination, the proxy tier is also responsible for authentication services. Chapter 8 describes what authentication options are available in SwiftStack.

SwiftStack clusters can be configured with additional authentication integrations with the SwiftStack Controller. Here are additional authentication options available with SwiftStack:

SwiftStack Auth: A fast, flat-file is deployed on each node with hashed passwords. This does not require a proxy restart. Users can be added via Controller web-interface. REST API is used to programmatically add/remove users. Great for application development, where there are a relatively fixed number of accounts on the clusters.

Keystone Auth: Enables Keystone to integrate with an OpenStack compute deployment.

Active Directory: Enables Active Directory for the cluster to participate in the AD domain.

LDAP: Enables LDAP authentication, for integration with an OpenLDAP service.

SWAuth: Uses the Swift cluster itself to store account data.

CSAuth: Enables integration with CloudStack.

Proxy Node Caching

While the proxy node does not cache objects, it does use its cache to store other data to improve performance. For example, the proxy nodes:

- Cache information about an account including the list of its containers.
- Cache container data – list of its objects and access-control list information.
- Store cname lookups so that an account url can be mapped to a hostname.
- Store static web data (index, css, for example).
- Store authentication tokens.
- Keep track of client requests when rate limiting is enabled.

Proxy Hardware

The proxy nodes use a moderate amount of RAM and are network I/O intensive. Typically, proxy servers are 1U systems with a minimum of 12 GB RAM. For small Swift clusters, the storage services and proxy services can run on the same physical nodes.

As these systems field each incoming API request, it is wise to provision them with two high-throughput (10GbE) interfaces. One interface is used for 'front-end,' incoming requests and the other for 'back-end' access to the storage nodes to put and fetch data.

For proxy nodes, we recommend the following specifications:

CPU – 64-bit x86 CPU (Intel/AMD), quad-core or greater, running at least 2-2.5GHz
RAM – 24 GB of RAM
Drives – Boot-drive only
Network

- 2 x 10 GbE recommended
- 1 x 1 GbE out-of-band management (IPMI/iLO)
- 1 x 1 GbE for in-band management and route to Controller

The Storage Tier

The storage tier in a Swift cluster is, naturally, where all the data resides. This tier runs all the storage services for the cluster. These include:

- Services to store and serve accounts, containers, and objects.
- Replication services for accounts, containers, and objects.
- Auditing processes for accounts, containers, and objects.
- Auditors to keep containers and accounts up-to-date.

Usable vs. Raw Storage Capacity

To calculate the usable versus raw storage capacity in your storage tier, there are a few considerations and it's a little bit more complicated than just dividing by '3'. To start, drive manufacturers label their drives with base 10 and operating systems use base 2! Additionally, there is some loss due to formatting a filesystem. All told there is a loss of about 8-9% to convert from the "marketing" size to something an operating system can use.

100 TB Example

To illustrate, let's go over an example that will yield 100 TB.

For 100 TB usable storage, we need 300 TB of 'formatted space' as Swift stores 3 replicas.

100TB * 3 Replicas = 300 TB

Then account for "marketing" vs. "actual" & disk formatting. 8% is a good number

300 TB * 1.08 = 324 TB

For this example, we will need a total of 324 TB of "marketing" TB.

Currently the 3TB drives offer a good price/density ratio.

So, for 324 TB needed / 3 TB drives = 108 drives

The next thing we need to consider is how many drives can conveniently fit into a storage chassis. One common form-factor we use has room for 36 storage drives. This would mean that we would need:

108 drives / 36 drive-bay node = 3 nodes for 100TB of storage.

Storage Hardware

Object storage nodes are typically configured as high-density 3U or 4U nodes with 16-36 SATA disks each. These nodes use a reasonable amount of memory and CPU. The storage nodes run services not only to field incoming requests from the proxy nodes, but also for replication, auditing and other processes to ensure durability. Storage nodes can be provisioned with single gigabit or 10GbE network interface depending on expected workload and desired performance.

For storage nodes, we recommend the following specifications:

CPU – 64-bit x86 CPU (Intel/AMD), quad-core or greater, running at least 2-2.5GHz

RAM – A good rule of thumb is approximately 0.5 GB of RAM for each TB of Disk. So, for a node with 24 drives, 36-48GB of RAM should be used. In addition to supporting the services, the system RAM will be used to cache the XFS inodes and buffer cache to quickly serve frequently accessed objects.

Drives – Either 3TB or 4TB 7200 RPM SATA drives, which deliver good price/performance value. Since the system does not use RAID, each request for an object is handled by a single disk. Subsequently, faster drives will increase the single-threaded response rates. Desktop-grade drives or enterprise-grade drives can be used. SwiftStack does not recommend using "green" drives as Swift is continuously ensuring data integrity and the power-down functions of green drives may result in excess wear.

Extreme container update workload consideration – Where the application needs to ingest many millions of files in a single container, it may be necessary to use higher-performing media such as SSDs for the container indexes. The data set is relatively very small in size, so not much space is needed on the higher performing media to store this data.

Controller Cards – Swift replicates data across zones so there is no need for data redundancy to be provided by the controller. Swift therefore uses standard SATA controller cards without RAID, such as LSI 9211-8i 6Gb/s SAS / SATA HBA. However, if the controller card requires RAID volumes to be created, set up a RAID 0 group (without striping) for each drive.

Network Cards – Depending on the use case, single gigabit ethernet (1GbE) on each host may be all that is required. However, it is possible to configure bonded 1GbE or 10GbE if the workload demands it.

Accounts and Container Tier

Each account and container is an individual SQLite database that is distributed across the cluster. An account database contains the list of containers in that account. A container database contains the list of objects in that container. To keep track of object data location, each account in the system has a database that references all its containers, and each container database references each object.

When your application needs to ingest many millions of files in a single container, it may be necessary to use higher-performing media,such as SSDs for the account and container metadata. The accounts and container data set is relatively small in size and does not require much storage, which makes it suitable to store on higher performing media, such as SSDs.

In most deployments, it is not required to configure a separate tier with the accounts and container metadata. To ensure that account and container listings are quick, SwiftStack recommends to add a pair of SSDs in each storage node for the account and metadata and configure SwiftStack to only store the account and container metadata on those SSDs. For very large deployments, the accounts and container metadata can be set up in an altogether different tier, with dedicated high-performance nodes (with SSDs).

Networking

A typical SwiftStack deployment will have an 'outward-facing' network (to run the proxy and authentication services) and an internal, 'cluster-facing' network. When designing the network capacity, keep in mind that writes fan-out in triplicate in the storage network. As there are three copies of each object, an incoming write is sent to three storage nodes. Therefore network capacity for writes needs to be considered in proportion to overall workload.

Starting from the client's perspective, the "client facing" IP would be the IP address (or DNS A record) that a client would connect to. Typically, that would be a WAN IP on a load balancer or on a firewall.

The "outward-facing" IP(s) would be the IP(s) on the proxy node(s). In some cases the proxy nodes could have public (WAN) IP addresses, but for security reasons we would typically not recommend that. The outward-facing IPs would thus be the IPs that get included in the load balancing pool.

The "cluster-facing" IP(s) would be IP(s) on which the proxies talk to the storage nodes, as well as the subnet on which storage nodes talk to each other.

For a small cluster, this could all be collapsed into having all nodes do everything. It is common that a smaller PoC installation has every node perform every task, using a 'Cluster API IP address.' But the sample deployments (below) will run through some different networking configurations.

Sample Deployments

So let's review some sample deployments for a SwiftStack cluster.

Small Cluster with 20TB of Usable Storage

For a small deployment with 2 nodes and a total of 20TB of usable storage, the SwiftStack packages will run all services on all nodes. This includes load balancing, proxy server, and object storage. This is automatically configured on the node through the SwiftStack installation and configuration process and does not require any additional setup by the operator.

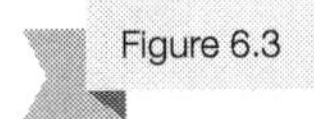

Small Cluster

RACK 1

Node 1:
- Load balancing
- Proxy service
- Object storage service

Node 1:
- Load balancing
- Proxy service
- Object storage service

- 2 SwiftStack nodes
- 12 drives in each node
- 3TB drives
- 72 TB of raw storage
- Approximately 20TB of usable storage

Medium Sized Cluster with 100TB of Usable Storage

For a medium sized deployment with 6-12 storage nodes, the cluster should be configured as follows:

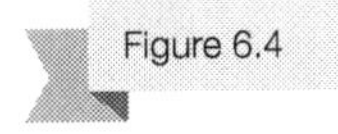

Medium Cluster

RACK 1

Node 1:
- Load balancing
- Proxy service

Node 2:
- Load balancing
- Proxy service

Node 3:
- Object storage service

Node 4:
- Object storage service

Node 7:
- Object storage service

- 2 proxy nodes
- 5 storage nodes
- 12 drives in each node
- 3TB drives
- 360 TB of raw storage
- Approximately 100TB of usable storage

At this scale, you could choose to run either a dedicated proxy/load balancing tier, or run all the services on every node.

If running a separate proxy tier, you should have at least two dedicated proxy/load balancing nodes for high-availability. The proxy nodes should also contain two interfaces, one for front-facing API requests and one "back-end" network connecting the storage nodes.

If you are running all services on each node, be sure to evaluate that the overall network capacity is suitable for your workload.

Typically, a single network tier is used for small and medium sized deployments. Either 1GbE or 10GbE switches can be used for this purpose depending on the throughput the cluster is expected to sustain.

Large Cluster with 1PB of Usable Storage

For larger deployments such as a cluster with 1PB of usable storage as detailed in the example below, you should consider the following:

- A separate load balancing tier may need to be used depending on the request throughput.
- The proxy nodes will be set up in a separate proxy tier. In this case, there are 8 proxy nodes.
- Each rack with storage nodes will be configured as a separate zone. In this example, there are 40 storage nodes, configured as 4U chassis with 36 3TB drives each. The zone can be configured in the SwiftStack Controller on the Node configuration page.
- A pair of aggregation switches with two links back to the front-end network / border network connects to the proxy tier and to each of the five top-of-rack(ToR) switches for each of the storage zones. All connections to the proxy tier and the zones are 10GbE
- In each rack with the storage nodes there is a pair of top-of-rack (ToR) switches. Each ToR switch connects to the aggregation network. Depending on overall concurrency desired, a deployment can use either a 1GbE or a 10GbE network to the object stores. It's possible to use a single, non-redundant switch as the system is designed to sustain a zone failure.

Figure 6.5 ***Large Cluster***

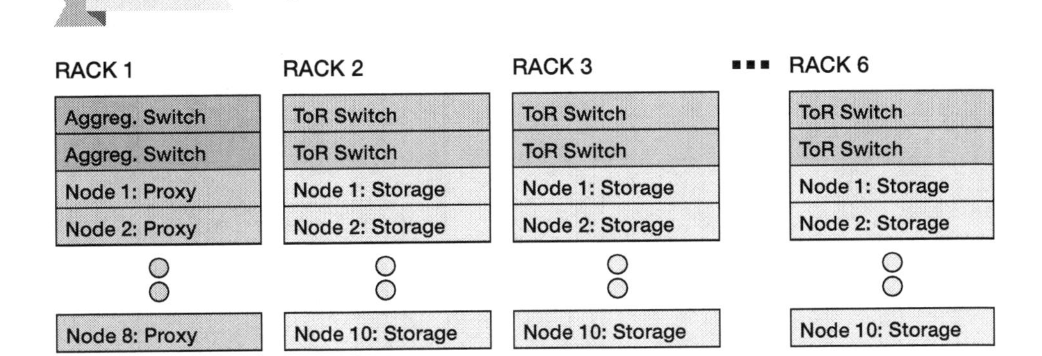

Creating a Tiered Swift Cluster

To illustrate how a SwiftStack cluster can be configured, let's walk through a step-by-step example of how to configure a SwiftStack cluster in two tiers: one proxy tier and one storage tier. The chart below shows how it could be set up.

Figure 6.6 ***Swift Cluster***

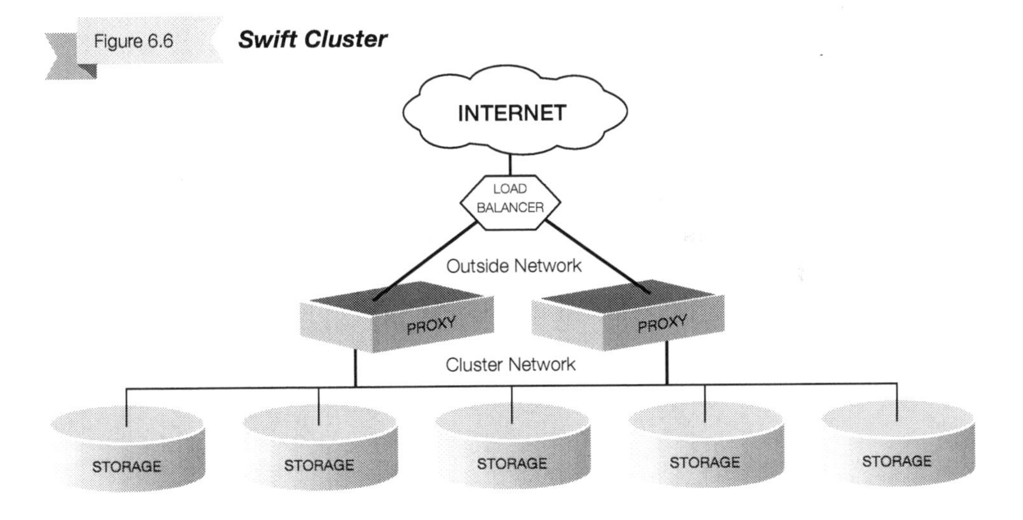

Sample Network Topology

You can run everything on one flat network, but it is generally better to separate external and internal traffic in the cluster. The following is an example of a network topology:

- The 'Outward-facing' network is the network which handles incoming traffic.
- The 'Cluster-facing' network is the internal network which takes care of replication traffic.

Network Schema

You can set up your network as follows:

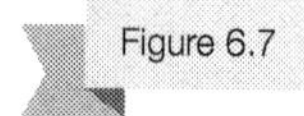
Figure 6.7

Description	Subnet	Netmask
Outward-facing	192.168.50.0	/24
Cluster-facing	192.168.51.0	/24

IP Address Assignments

For this example we will be using two (2) proxy nodes and three (3) storage nodes.

Figure 6.8

Node Name	Outward IP Address	Cluster IP Addr
proxy1	192.168.50.11	192.168.50.11
proxy2	192.168.50.12	192.168.50.12
storage1	192.168.51.101	192.168.51.101
storage2	192.168.51.102	192.168.51.102
storage3	192.168.51.103	192.168.51.103

Load Balancing

SwiftStack includes a load balancer that can be used with very little configuration. The SwiftStack load balancer is based on the LVS open source project. The SwiftStack load balancer binds to a single node and routes requests to each of the other SwiftStack proxy nodes.

For workloads that exceed the capability of the SwiftStack load balancer, we recommend using a dedicated load balancing product, such as an F5 or A10. Please contact us (*contact@swiftstack.com*) for specific recommendations.

With an external load balancer any load balancing method may be used, such as simple round robin DNS or a layer 4 or layer 7 load balancer. The type of load balancing you chose depends on your use-case and what your cluster workload will look like. Selecting and setting up the load balancing solution is therefore up to you. SwiftStack has worked with customers who have used everything from round robin DNS using BIND, HAProxy and other open source solutions, as well as commercial equipment from companies like f5 and A10.

Configuring The SwiftStack Load Balancer

Setting up the SwiftStack load balancer is very easy. Simply check the box for `Use SwiftStack Load Balancer` to enable it and make sure to use a different IP address than what you are using for your nodes.

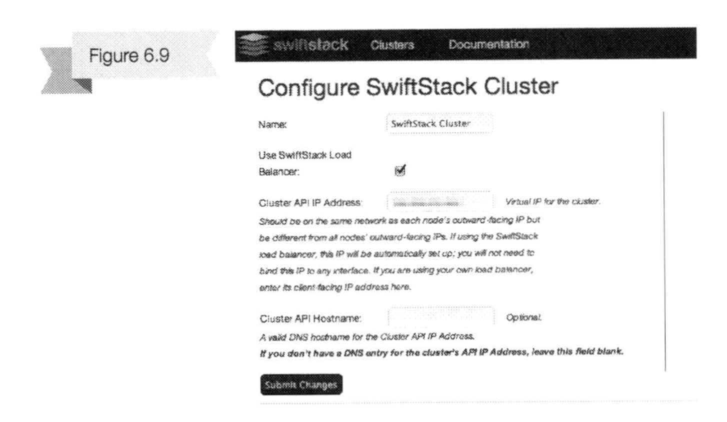

Figure 6.9

Configuring An External Load Balancer

If you are setting up a cluster with an external load balancer, you will need to set up your load balancer to divide the load between your proxy nodes.

Using the network topology example provided above, if you have selected 192.168.50.0/24 as your 'Outward-facing' network, you need to set up your load balancer to include the IP addresses of the proxy nodes in its load balancing pool. You will also need to assign the load balancer a virtual IP (VIP) on which it will respond. Here we will use 192.168.50.10 for the VIP. So, for this example, the IP addresses used would be as follows:

- 192.168.50.10 (load balancer VIP)
- 192.168.50.11 (proxy1, included in pool)
- 192.168.50.12 (proxy2, included in pool)

To configure the external load balancer to pull failing nodes out of the load balancing pool, configure the load balancer to use the proxy node's health check URL.

The health check URL in our example would be:

- *http://192.168.50.11/healthcheck*
- *http://192.168.50.12/healthcheck*

Node Naming Conventions
It is good practice to name the nodes in a way that makes it simple to to distinguish between proxy and storage nodes. For small clusters, just naming the nodes, as in the example above – proxy1, storage1 and so forth – is usually good enough. However, for larger clusters, it may be good to expand on the naming convention schema. Below is an example of how you might name nodes in a larger cluster:

- Data Center (d)
- Cluster (c)
- Rack (r)
- Node (n)
- Proxy (p)
- Zone (z) [optional]

Examples:
d1-c1-r2-n3.example.com
d1-c1-r2-p1.example.com

Proxy Nodes
The proxy nodes do not need storage other than for the OS drive(s). To install a proxy node follow the same process as installing a storage node. For details on how to install a SwiftStack node, please see the section on installing a SwiftStack node in Chapter 4 (Installing OpenStack Swift). For more detailed install instructions see *http://swiftstack.com/docs/install-guide/.*

If you have two proxy nodes assign the network interfaces as follows:

- proxy1:
  'Outward-facing' interface: 192.168.50.11
  'Cluster-facing' interface: 192.168.51.11
- proxy2:
  'Outward-facing' interface: 192.168.50.12
  'Cluster-facing' interface: 192.168.51.12

The two proxies are now ready to be deployed. Incoming requests to the cluster will be routed through the load balancing solution to the proxies and from the proxies to the storage nodes, as depicted in the diagram at the beginning of this section.

Storage Nodes

For storage nodes you will need hard disks for Swift to store your data. Other than the inclusion of hard disks for storage, the SwiftStack node installation is the same as described above. However, the configuration is a bit different. Only the proxy nodes will be included in the load balancer's proxy pool, which means incoming requests will only be forwarded to the proxy nodes. So, the storage nodes don't need to listen to the outward-facing subnet. Therefore, instead of using the 192.168.50.0/24 subnet for the 'Outward-facing' interface, you can use the cluster-facing, 192.168.51.0/24 subnet for both interfaces on the storage nodes.
For example:

- storage1:
  'Outward-facing' interface: 192.168.51.101
  'Cluster-facing' interface: 192.168.51.101
- storage2:
  'Outward-facing' interface: 192.168.51.102
  'Cluster-facing' interface: 192.168.51.102
- storage3:
  'Outward-facing' interface: 192.168.51.103
  'Cluster-facing' interface: 192.168.51.103

The last thing you need to do to your storage nodes is to configure the storage layout of your drives. If you only have traditional, spinning disks in your cluster, you can format and add all the disks in the same way. If, however, you have opted to use an SSD for your account and container data, your disk configuration will be slightly different. With an SSD in the hardware configuration, instead of putting account, container, and object data on all drives, you would configure your storage layout with account and container data on the SSD and the object data on regular hard disks. A simple configuration for these two scenarios could look something like this:

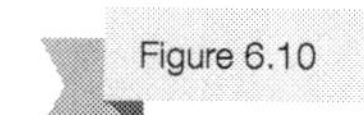

Figure 6.10 ***Only regular hard disks***

Label	Device	Size (GB)	Type	Account/Container Ring Status	Object Ring Status
d1	sdb	2000	xfs	In Use	In Use
d2	sdc	2000	xfs	In Use	In Use
d3	sdd	2000	xfs	In Use	In Use
d4	sde	2000	xfs	In Use	In Use

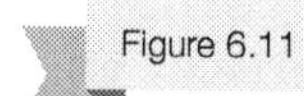

Figure 6.11 ***SSD + hard disks***

Label	Device	Size (GB)	Type	Account/Container Ring Status	Object Ring Status
d1	sdb	148	xfs	In Use	Ready
d2	sdc	2000	xfs	Ready	In Use
d3	sdd	2000	xfs	Ready	In Use
d4	sde	2000	xfs	Ready	In Use

Note: The the top row is highlighted to indicate SSD.

Push Config to Cluster

When your proxy and storage nodes have their IP addresses configured and you have configured the drive, it's time to `Push Config to Cluster`. The configuration push will deliver all the Swift rings to each of the nodes and make them ready to receive data. The configuration push can take some time, so be patient while the ring configuration is created and deployed to your cluster.

Additional Notes on Tiered Clusters

Below are a few additional notes on tiered Swift clusters. None of the settings described below are necessary for tiering to work. Only make the changes below if you have a strong reason for doing so, or if SwiftStack support has suggested that you do.

- In a tiered cluster all the processes for proxy, account, container, and objects are of course still running on the server. This does take some extra RAM, but because the proxy processes on the storage nodes are not actually used, no CPU resources will be taken by the proxy processes.

- If you want to ensure that storage nodes do not respond to Swift's "healthcheck" feature, you can disable the Swift healthcheck by touching a file on each of your storage nodes. Doing so will set the healthcheck in a disabled state and the system will not try to include it among its proxies. To create (touch) the file you need to log in via SSH on the node and issue the following command:

```
$ sudo touch /etc/swift/PROXY-HEALTCHECK-DISABLED-503
```

- If you find that using the same IP address for the 'Outward-facing' and 'Cluster-facing' interfaces on the storage nodes is confusing, you can also use a third network, like 192.168.52.0/24 for the 'Outward-facing' interface on the storage nodes.

Creating a Globally Distributed Cluster

In the "Grizzly" release of Swift, several new features are being introduced which make it possible to deploy a single Swift cluster over multiple, geographically distant locations. Some of these new features include:

Region tier in the ring - This features enables the existing "unique-as-possible" placement strategy to continue to work across a distributed cluster and ensures that data is as protected from failures as possible. A region is bigger than a zone and extends the concept of tiered zones. Each storage node can be placed in a region.

Adjustable replica count - When adding regions to a cluster, the number of replicas will need to be equal to at least as many regions are configured in the cluster. This features lets operators add and remove replicas based on how many regions are configured.

Dedicated replication network support - This feature will allow replication traffic between storage nodes over a separate network.

Proxy affinity - With this feature, proxy servers can choose local replicas for reads. In a single region, this may mean that a replica in the same server or same rack (e.g. zone) is chosen. For multi-region, this means that reads are sent to the local region first instead of geographically distant replicas.

Multi region replication - Allows replicas to be stored in multiple physical regions.

These additional features in Swift will enable an operator to configure and deploy clusters that can support several additional use-cases, including:

Offsite Disaster Recovery (DR) - One replica is stored in a geographically distant datacenter apart from the other replicas for disaster recovery purposes.

Multi-site sharing - Suitable for deployments where each geographic region would be accessed equally. This would be ideal for multi-site archiving and file sharing applications.

Active-Active Access - Suitable for a dual-coast deployment where each location is accessed equally heavily. For example, a web/mobile application that is delivering application assets and content to multiple locations.

To create a globally distributed cluster, storage nodes are deployed in each region. The proxy nodes will have an affinity to a region and be able to optimistically write to storage nodes based on the storage nodes' region. The client will have the option to perform a write or read that goes across regions (ignoring local affinity), if required.

Let's look at some examples of how these features can be configured:

Offsite Disaster Recovery (DR)

This configuration would be good for having two replicas in a single region (the 'primary' location) and using another region to have a single replica (the 'offsite' location).

When a client makes a request to the 'primary' region, the proxy node will prioritize the storage nodes in its region over remote regions allowing for higher throughput and lower latency on storage requests. For uploads, as usual, three replicas will be written in unique locations, but the proxy node will select three locations in the same region. Then, the replicators will asynchronously replicate one of the three copies to the 'offsite' region.

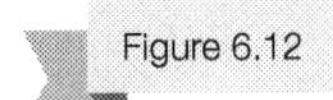

Offsite DR with 2 Regions and 3 Replicas

Asynchronous offsite replica / High-throughput upload

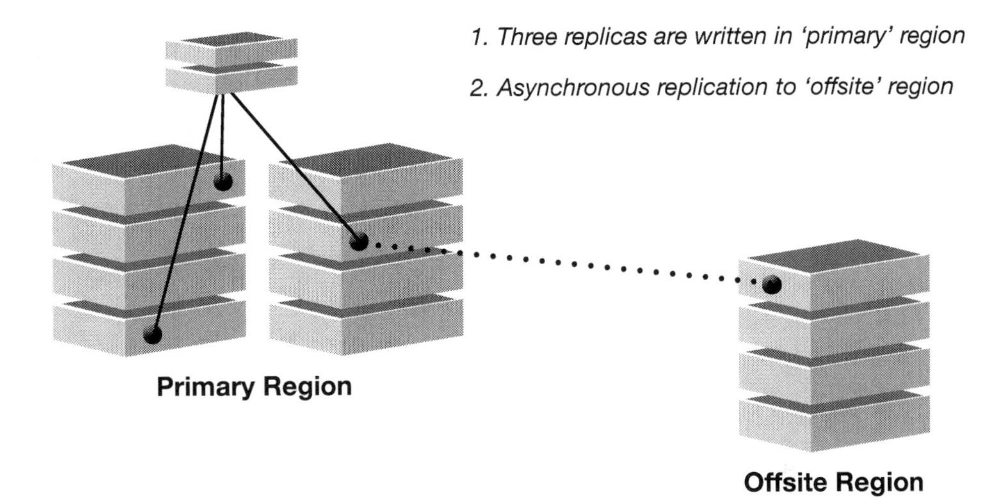

3. Two copies in 'primary', one copy in 'offsite' region

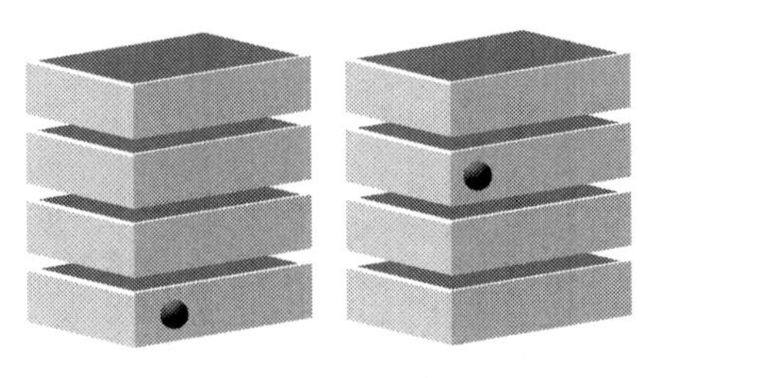

To provide a fully-replicated write at the expense of a higher-latency upload the client could force a concurrent write across the two regions. Similarly, the client could use the current 'fetch newest' feature to force the proxy node to check timestamps of all replicas (including those from the 'offsite' region) to determine the best copy to return.

Multi-site Sharing

This use case would be suitable for deployments where each geographic region would be accessed equally. This would be ideal for multi-site archiving and file sharing applications.

Each site would accept writes and write three copies 'as-unique-as-possible' within the region. Then, asynchronously, the object would be replicated to the other regions. The client would be provided a more conservative write option to perform a concurrent write across all regions.

Figure 6.13 **_Multi-site Sharing with 3 Regions and 3 Replicas_**
Asynchronous offsite replica / High-throughput upload

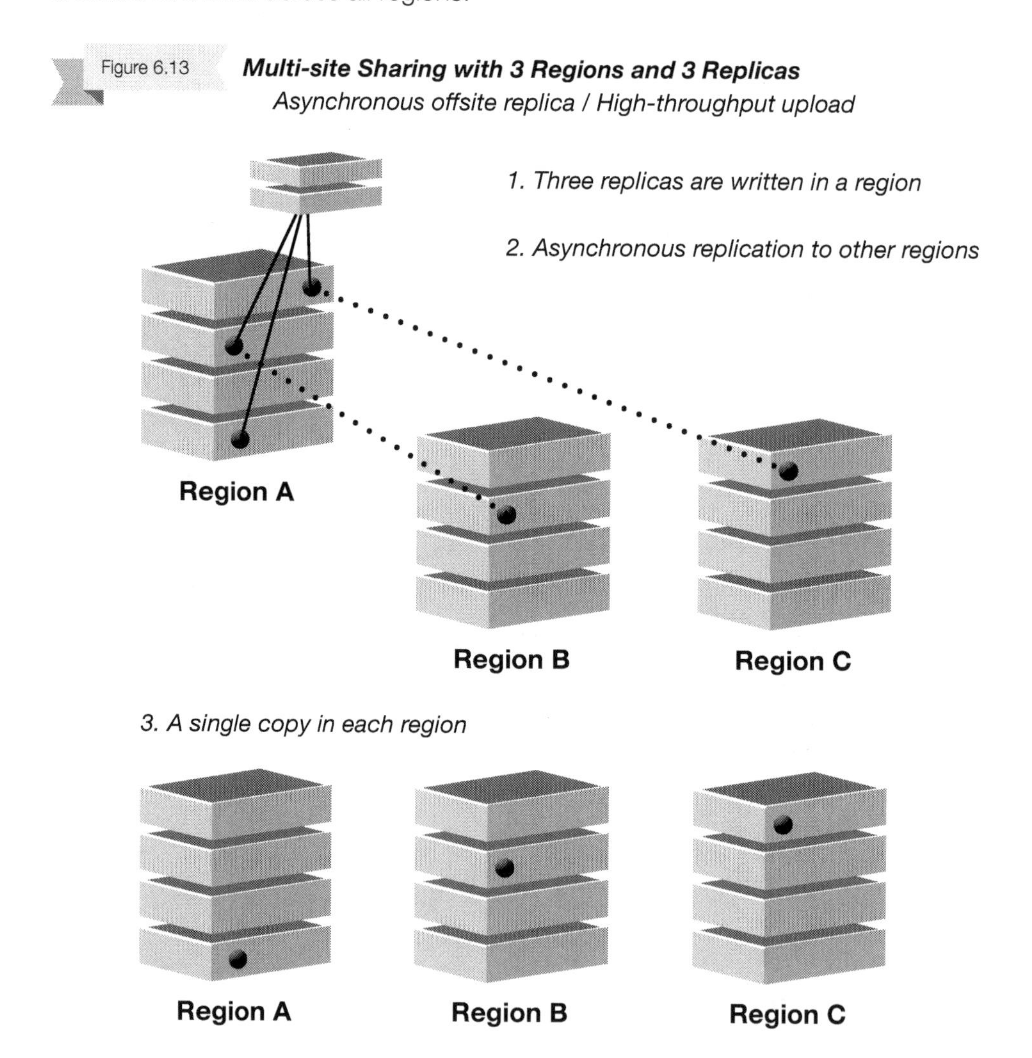
1. Three replicas are written in a region
2. Asynchronous replication to other regions
Region A
Region B
Region C
3. A single copy in each region
Region A
Region B
Region C

A client would read from a local region and there would be an affinity to serve data from a storage node within the region. A client would also be provided with the ability to 'fetch newest', where the proxy node would query each region to determine the newest object based on their timestamps.

Active/Active Access

This use case would be useful for a dual-coast deployment where each location is accessed equally heavily. For example, a web/mobile application that is delivering application assets and content to multiple locations.

This would be similar to Offsite DR (see above) but it allows for increased availability in each region. In this use case, when the option to concurrently write to multiple regions is successful, that application asset can be used immediately in the application globally.

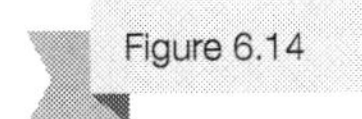

Active/Active Access with 2 Regions and 4 Replicas

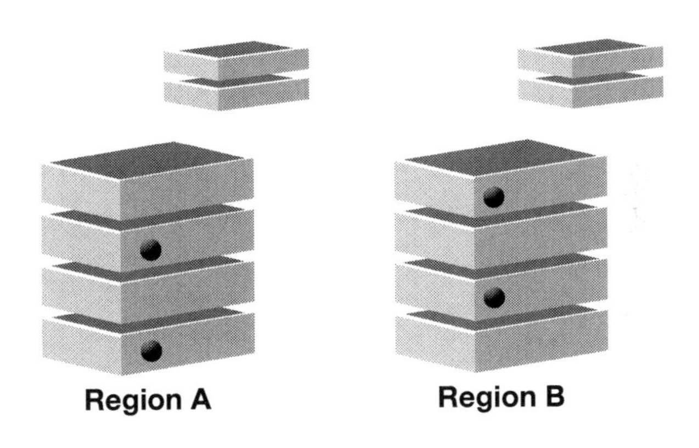

Conclusion

By now you've learned how to set up a Swift cluster. More importantly, you've learned how to make informed decisions pertaining to configuration, networking, naming of nodes, and load balancing. You also have seen how to create globally distributed clusters, if your use case demands. Next we'll turn to operating a Swift cluster (Chapter 7), integrating Swift (Chapter 8), testing and benchmarking (Chapter 9), and finally tuning (Chapter 10).

CHAPTER SEVEN

Operating a SwiftStack Cluster

In this chapter we move from installation to the everyday maintenance of a Swift-Stack Cluster. This is, in many ways, the heart of the book. We'll cover best practices for conducting day-to-day operational tasks, such as planning capacity additions; procedures for handling drive failures; monitoring, tuning and requesting technical support. The recommendations and best practices in this guide are based on our experience building and operating both large and small clusters for a variety of workloads. By the end of this chapter you'll understand how to operate a Swift cluster with SwiftStack!

Adding Capacity

Data is always growing and disk capacity is always increasing. SwiftStack makes the process of adding and removing capacity easy and highly automated. When capacity needs to grow, you won't have to ramp-up your knowledge on ring-building tactics. SwiftStack also keeps track of your cluster so you won't make mistakes when adding capacity. When the time comes and the old equipment isn't pulling its weight, SwiftStack makes sure that the retiring hardware exits the cluster gracefully.

How Swift Distributes Data

To understand how to best add capacity to a SwiftStack cluster, it is important to first understand how Swift places data. Swift distributes data in cluster locations that are "as unique-as-possible." With this data placement feature, Swift can intelligently place data on any storage device in the cluster, preferring locations that are in different zones, nodes, and disks. All data stored in Swift also has two "handoff" locations defined, which are alternative data placement locations in the cluster, should one of the three replicas not be available, due to hardware or other failure.

When you add more capacity to a Swift cluster data will be re-distributed evenly across cluster resources, including newly added drives. For instance, if the cluster is 80% full and you're adding a new node or a new rack without any data, the Swift cluster will level itself so all drives will have an equal amount of data stored on them. For a large cluster, this may not be noticeable but for a small cluster, this additional replication traffic needs to be managed to ensure it does not negatively impact performance of the cluster. It is therefore important to let the data flow into the new capacity you've added at a moderate rate and not at the bottleneck rate of the network.

Adding Capacity with the SwiftStack Controller

When you add new capacity to a SwiftStack cluster, such as additional disk drives, the SwiftStack Controller automates the process by:

- Detecting new devices that are added to a node
- Labeling drives with a unique label, so they can be mounted, unmounted, and remounted without losing their identity in the process
- Mounting the drives
- Formatting the drives with the XFS filesystem
- Adding the drives to the ring
- Deploying the new ring to all cluster nodes

While the SwiftStack Controller automates the process of adding additional capacity, the operator still needs to manage and plan for capacity additions - and pay attention to how full existing drives are. A good rule of thumb is to keep at least 10-20% free on all drives, which provides some headroom for future capacity needs and gives you the time to order and install additional drives or nodes.

Adding Drives

To add additional drives to an existing node in a SwiftStack cluster install the physical drives in the node and follow these steps:

Step 1:	In the SwiftStack Controller, go to `Configure Cluster` and then `Edit` the node you have added the drives. Note that the SwiftStack Controller will automatically detect additional drives in the cluster.
Step 2:	Either add all drives on the node `Gradually` or `Now` to your cluster.
Step 3:	Press `Change`.
Step 4:	"Push the Config" to the cluster.

With SwiftStack, you can add additional capacity, such as new drives, automatically into your existing clusters, with two different options: `Add Gradually` and `Add Now`. With `Add Gradually`, the SwiftStack Controller will slowly increment the weights on each new device, rebalance, and safely distribute the ring out to all the nodes. The SwiftStack Controller will also track information about replication activity so it knows when to do the next increment. On the node monitoring page, you can track the percent complete for each device.

With `Add Now`, the SwiftStack Controller will add the new cluster resources immediately, which will result in replication traffic to evenly redistribute the data across the cluster.

To determine if `Add Gradually` or `Add Now` is most appropriate, the following guidelines may provide a starting point:

- If > 20% capacity is added, `Add Gradually` is probably most appropriate
- If < 20% capacity is added, `Add Now` may be ok

This, however, varies based on:

- Actual size of cluster
- Percentage added
- Workload cluster is under

For a cluster with more than a few dozen drives, it is typically ok to `Add Now`. When adding a new node, however, it may be more appropriate to `Add Gradually`.

Adding a Node

To add a new node to an existing SwiftStack cluster, install the SwiftStack Node software on the node as described in the latter half of the 'Installing OpenStack Swift' chapter.

To determined whether you should `Add Gradually` or `Add Immediately` and for a reminder about how you can monitor the process see the previous section (Adding Drives).

The SwiftStack Controller will add the newly available capacity into the cluster.

Removing Capacity

SwiftStack also makes it easy to remove capacity from a cluster, which you'll need to do when you want to upgrade to larger drives, swap out older drives, or replace a whole node. The process for removing capacity is similar to adding capacity. But instead of `Add Gradually`, you can `Remove Gradually` and then wait until all data has been removed from the disk(s) or node(s) so you can remove them from the cluster.

Removing a Node

The following procedures can be used when it is necessary to remove a node from a cluster. You may need to remove a node when upgrading hardware; when you've experienced hardware failure; or when you're conducting operational and failure testing of a SwiftStack cluster. When conducting operational and failure testing these procedures will enable you to safely simulate node and disk failures without potentially damaging the hardware by actually, physically removing disks or forcing servers to shut down by a hard power off event.

To safely remove a node from a SwiftStack cluster, do the following:

Step 1:	Gracefully shut down the node: `$ sudo shutdown -h now` **NOTE:** The node will shut down and the SwiftStack Controller will show the node as unreachable. When a node is down, Swift assumes that the disks are still healthy and that the data on those disks is recoverable. Consequently, if the node is powered back on, Swift will simply bring the node back into the cluster and will start syncing any new data to the node.
Step 2:	Delete the node from the SwiftStack Controller's GUI. When the node is deleted from the controller, a ring push will be initiated, which will completely remove the node from the cluster.

Removing a Drive

If a drive has failed or is having issues, or if you want to replace a disk with a larger disk to increase capacity you'll need to remove it and replace it with a new drive.

Disks can be removed in two ways: `Now` (immediately) or `Gradually`.

If a disk is removed using the `Now` button, it is immediately removed from the cluster and the data remains on the disk.

If a disk is removed `Gradually`, data will be slowly removed from the drive and transferred to other disks in the cluster. The cluster will try to remove 25GB/hour from the disk. Thus, removing data completely from a drive with 2TB of data on it will take approximately 80 hours, or close to 3.5 days. However, if the cluster is under heavy load or busy with other processes, it may drain less than 25GB of data per hour, which would make the removal process slower than calculated above.

During a gradual removal of a drive, what happens is that the weight of the drive is gradually reduced by 25GB/hour, which forces data to be reallocated to other disks in the cluster. So, every hour there is a new ring pushed to the cluster, which triggers a rebalancing of the disks in the cluster.

If, for any reason, a configuration push cannot be completed and the ring cannot be updated, the gradual removal of data will be interrupted. For example, if a node goes down and is not repaired and reinstated or removed from the cluster, the ring updating cannot continue until the cluster is healthy again. The gradual removal of data will continue once a new ring can be pushed to the cluster.

To remove a disk `Now`, In the SwiftStack Controller's GUI, follow these instructions:

Step 1:	Go to the node from which you want to remove the disk.
Step 2:	Click on the `Manage` button.
Step 3:	Find the disk you want to remove, for example *sde*.
Step 4:	From the dropdown menu, select `Remove Immediately`. The disk will be instantly deleted from the cluster and a configuration push will be initiated to rebalance the cluster.

To remove a disk `Gradually`, in the SwiftStack Controller, follow these instructions:

Step 1:	Go to the node from which you want to remove the disk.
Step 2:	Click on the `Manage` button.
Step 3:	Find the disk you want to remove, for example *sde*.
Step 4:	From the dropdown menu, select `Remove Gradually`.

After removing a disk from a node, if you later want to re-use the disk in the cluster, you should ensure that the data on the disk is removed so that it looks like a new disk to Swift. One way of removing all data is to simply format the disk.

Cleaning Up a Disk

If you are planning on adding a disk that has previously been part of the cluster back to the cluster, it may be required to first re-format it to ensure that any data on the disk is removed. This procedure is especially useful when conducting operational and failure testing of a cluster.

Step 1:	From the command line, unmount the disk sde mounted on */srv/node/d3:* `$ sudo umount /srv/node/d3`
Step 2:	Now, format the disk: `$ sudo mkfs.xfs -f -i size=512 /dev/sde`
Step 3:	The disk should now be ready for use again, as if it was a brand new disk.

Once you have cleaned up the disk as described above, you can re-add it to the node and it will appear to the SwiftStack Controller as a new disk.

Handling Hardware Failures

All clusters will at some point experience a hardware failure. Hardware failures can come in many forms - whole drives can become unresponsive, a power supply to a node can can fail, a switch can break and/or parts of the cluster, such as a rack, can experience a power outage. Fortunately, Swift is designed to withstand hardware failures - small and large. A Swift cluster can operate without impact to the durability and availability of the data even with failed drives, nodes, or even whole racks.

By default, SwiftStack places data in cluster locations that are "as unique-as-possible", which makes it easier to deploy small clusters and provides great durability when the cluster experiences a hardware failure. With this data placement feature, Swift can intelligently place data on any storage device in the cluster, preferring locations that are in different zones, nodes, and disks. All data stored in SwiftStack also has two "handoff" locations defined, which are alternative data placement locations in the cluster should one of the three replicas not be available due to a hardware failure. It is important to note that drives in a Swift cluster are *not* mirrored and are not configured with RAID. This means that when there is a hardware failure, such as a drive failure, the entire cluster will participate in the replication of the data to handoff locations. There are no RAID re-builds, which could cripple the performance of the cluster.

Handling a Failed Drive

A drive failure in Swift is not an emergency event. Should an individual drive in a cluster fail, the following will happen automatically, without requiring any intervention by the operator:

1. The SwiftStack Controller console will alert the operator of the drive failure as a Missing Device in the alerts dashboard.
2. A drive failure will trigger replication.

Note that when a drive fails, it will become unmounted and this will indicate to Swift that the drive has failed. Then the replicators for all of those objects on different servers will detect that one of the objects replicas is unavailable due to the drive failure. Now replication to the handoff node will be triggered. In effect this means that when your drive becomes unmounted that data suddenly has two replicas in the cluster but replicators will immediately get to those objects in the replication pass. This will replicate the object, so there are once again three replicas in the cluster. Also, unlike RAID systems, Swift does not require any re-build time when a failed drive is replaced. Since the entire cluster participates in the replication of data that was stored on the failed drive, the cluster will quickly replicate the data that was stored on the failed drive to handoff locations in the cluster, always ensuring that the number of replicas remain constant.

Procedure for handling drive failures:

Step 1:	**Acknowledge the alert in the Controller** To acknowledge and archive an alert, click the `Acknowledge Alert` button. That alert will be removed from the count of alerts that appear on the top of the page. To acknowledge and archive all alerts, click the `Archive All Alerts` button.
Step 2:	**Remove failed drive in Controller** In the SwiftStack Controller, you can remove the disk from the cluster. This will operationally remove the disk from the cluster. Use this option if you will not be getting to the data center in a reasonable timeframe. If the disk is 'dying', use the `Remove Gradually` option, if the disk has failed and is not responsive, use the Remove `Immediately` option.
Step 3:	**Replace the failed drive in physical node** The failed drive can normally be replaced during regularly scheduled maintenance periods. In other words, drive failure in Swift is not a critical event as the data on the drive has been re-created in handoff locations elsewhere in the cluster, thus always ensuring that the defined number of replicas exists. The replacement drive will be folded into the cluster (see the previous sections on Adding Capacity) and the cluster will re-distribute data in an even manner across cluster resources. See the section on Removing A Disk (below) for details.
Step 4:	**Format and add new drive in Controller** For details refer to the Adding Drives subsection (above).

Should a drive failure happen during an upload, the following will happen: When an object PUT comes in (an upload), the proxy server tries to stream that object out to three storage servers. Let's say this object is destined for a currently failed drive. When the node with the failed drive tries to write the object, it is going to report an error stating that the drive is failed.

Then the proxy server will receive that information and select a handoff location, which is determined in the ring. The ring will determine the next handoff locations for every single object. The proxy server will simply take the next hand off location for this particular object and try to send the replica there. That way the cluster will still have three replicas and the client will see a success.

Handling a Full Drive

Another scenario to consider is how to handle full drives, which can happen if enough capacity has not been added to the cluster to keep up with data growth. As Swift distributes data across the cluster *evenly*, the most full disks will correspond to how full the overall cluster is and when you should consider adding additional capacity. When a drive is full or close to full, it will be displayed in the `Top 5 Least Free Disks` in the main configuration page of the SwiftStack Controller.

Procedures for handling full hard drives:

Step 1:	Add additional hard drives. (Yes, that's it. Swift takes care of the rest.)

Handling Sector or Partial Drive Failure (a.k.a. bit-rot)

In a Swift cluster, auditing processes run continuously to ensure that all data is always available. It does this by "walking" each object on a given node to detect corruption, which is done in three different ways:

First, the auditing process will conduct a quick pass to check for zero-byte files. Leaving a zero-byte file is the way that the `XFS` file system notifies the operator that it has detected corruption.

Second, there is a slower-moving process which will recalculate each object's checksum and compare it to what Swift has for it on record. If the file is determined to be corrupt, it is moved to a quarantined location. Replication will trigger and a 'fresh' copy of the file will be replicated, replacing the corrupted copy.

Finally, as a stopgap, if the file is requested and a yet-to-be-detected corrupt file is returned to the client, Swift will recalculate the checksum as the file is being streamed to the client. If the checksum fails, the object is moved to the quarantine location. The client can then compare the checksum and refetch the object.

Should any of the above occur, Swift will automatically quarantine the specific objects, replicate the objects to handoff locations, and notify the operator via SwiftStack's alerts dashboard.

Handling Unreachable Nodes

Should an entire node become unreachable due to a power-failure, networking issue, or motherboard failure an alert will be generated in the SwiftStack Controller. SwiftStack continuously monitors if nodes are available in the cluster by detecting timeouts. There are 2 timeouts that check this - the connection timeout (.5 sec) and the node timeout (10 sec). Should a node be unavailable within these timeouts, the node will be reported as `Node is unreachable.`

When a node is unreachable, Swift assumes that the data is still available on the node but temporarily not accessible. Unlike when drive failures occur, Swift will not automatically attempt to replicate data to handoff locations as the failure is very likely caused by a networking issue or failed power supply in the node. This data is likely still available on the drives on the "failed" node, and it may be a simpler operation to make the repair and re-connect the node to the cluster instead of immediately replicating the data. New writes will continue to write 3 replicas.

At SwiftStack we uniquely ID the drives so that we can keep track of where each drive is expected to be mapped back into the Swift ring. One thing *not* to do is rely on */dev/sd<x>* location of drives. Often this becomes problematic because when there are hardware changes, the system will change the */dev/* location of each drive. Again, with SwiftStack this is handled automatically.

When there is a node failure, it is more critical than with drive failures for the operator to take action quickly to ensure that the desired availability level for the cluster is maintained.

Procedure for handling unreachable nodes:

Step 1:	**Acknowledge the alert** To acknowledge and archive an alert, click the `Acknowledge Alert` button. That alert will be removed from the count of alerts that appear on the top of the page. To acknowledge and archive all alerts, click the `Archive All Alerts` button.
Step 2:	**Do not make any cluster configuration changes in the Controller** It is important not to introduce other configuration changes in the cluster when dealing with hardware failures as that may introduce additional variables which may impact the operation of your cluster.

Step 3:	**Check network connectivity** In most cases, a networking issue causes a node to be temporarily unreachable. Investigate if the node is available on the network. Check switches, cables, networking cards etc. to ensure they work as they should. If a networking issue is indeed the root cause, the node can be re-connected with the cluster without any special procedures. Swift's consistency processes will ensure that data on all nodes in the cluster will be re-balanced and distributed evenly. Should the root cause be faulty hardware on the node itself, proceed to the next section (Handling a Failed Node). Otherwise, proceed to step 4.
Step 4:	**Re-connect node to the cluster** Swift's auditing process will automatically ensure that any changes to the data on the node since it was unreachable will be updated.

Handling a Failed Node

So what if you know this is a system that is never going to come back online? Say the motherboard burns out, the power supply fails, or the network becomes disconnected. What will Swift do? What do you as an operator need to do?

As mentioned earlier, what Swift *won't* do is replicate all of the data that's on that node (or zone/region) to handoff locations. What Swift *will* do is mark that node as failed and not attempt to upload any new data to it. New data will be sent to handoff locations to ensure that the cluster will still have three good replicas.

The logic behind not initiating replication, is that a node failure is much more likely to be caused by specific, transitory events and not by system catastrophes, such as fire or water damage. Given this, Swift will assume that the event was transitory and all the drives are not physically destroyed. Initiating replication on an entire node, zone, or region is a high cost operation and should only be initiated when you know that the data is physically gone.

But if you know that the data is gone, you need to do the following:

Step 1:	**Acknowledge the alert**
Step 2:	**Do not make any cluster configuration changes in the Controller**
Step 3:	**If node needs to be replaced or repaired for an extended period of time, remove node in Controller** In the SwiftStack Controller, select to remove all drives for the failed node either `Now` or `Gradually`. This will ensure that the cluster will re-create the data to handoff location so that you have 3 replicas of all your data. Selecting `Now` will result in an increase in replication traffic on your cluster, which may impact performance during replication. Selecting to remove all drives for the failed node `Gradually` will minimize any spikes in traffic resulting from the increase in replication traffic in your cluster, but will take a longer time to replicate the data from the failed node(s) to the handoff locations in the cluster.
Step 4:	**Replace physical node in datacenter**

Monitoring your SwiftStack cluster

A SwiftStack cluster has many moving parts - with many daemons running across many nodes, all working together. It is therefore important to be able to tell what's going on *inside* the cluster when diagnosing issues and performance or planning capacity changes. The SwiftStack Controller tracks not only server-level metrics like CPU utilization, load, memory consumption, disk usage, and utilization, but also hundreds of Swift specific metrics to understand what the different daemons are doing on each server. This helps the operator to answer questions such as, "What's the volume of object replication on node8?", "How long is it taking?", "Are there errors? If so, when did they happen?"

The SwiftStack Controller collects and stores monitoring data for over 500 metrics for each node in your SwiftStack cluster. A subset of these are reported in the SwiftStack Controller so you can get a bird's eye view of your cluster performance, with options to drill down into specific metrics for tuning and troubleshooting.

SwiftStack monitoring data is reported by StatsD, a simple stats deamon that runs on all Swift nodes. To avoid the problems inherent with middleware-based monitoring and after-the-fact log processing, StatsD metrics are integrated into Swift itself. With StatsD, metrics are sent in real-time from the nodes to the SwiftStack Controller. The overhead of sending a metric is extremely low: a sendto of one UDP packet.

Cluster Level Metrics

The SwiftStack Controller highlights the following top-level metrics in the Controller console for each cluster:

Cluster CPU Utilization	Measures the percentage of the time that a node is using the CPU or performing disk I/O. CPU utilization is provided both for the overall cluster and for individual nodes. High rates (e.g. above 80%) are generally bad. If your CPU utilization is high, processes may have a harder time getting resources. This means that processes on this node will start to slow down and that it may be time to add additional nodes to the cluster.
Cluster Proxy Throughput	Displayed in bytes/second. This is the aggregate throughput for all inbound and outbound traffic. This will indicate network bottlenecks if any exist.
Average Node Memory Utilization	This is the memory usage for all nodes in your cluster. Memory is displayed as either used, buffered, cached, or free.
Total Cluster Disk I/O	Measures the total number of Input/Output Operations Per Second (IOPS) on disks for the overall cluster and for individual nodes. Disk I/O is shown for both Read IOPS and Write IOPS. Note that since Swift constantly guards against bit-rot, the cluster will continuously read some amount of data.
Top 5 Least Free Disks	Displays the most full disks in the cluster. Swift distributes data across the cluster evenly so how full your disks are will correspond to how full the overall cluster is and when you should consider adding additional capacity.

The SwiftStack Controller also makes available several other monitoring graphs for your cluster, which are used when tuning or troubleshooting your SwiftStack cluster. For the overall cluster, these graphs include:

- Total Cluster Interface Bandwidth
- StatsD Statistics Per Node
- Avg OpenVPN Traffic
- Top 4 Avg Node Process Groups by RSS
- object-updater sweep Timing and Count
- object-replicator.partition.update Req Timing and Count
- Proxy Req Timing and Count
- account-replicator replication Timing and Count

Node Level Metrics

For each node, the following monitoring graphs are available:

- Total Node Disk I/O
- Per-Disk Read Throughput
- Per-Disk Write Throughput
- Per-Disk Read IOPs
- Per-Disk Write IOPs
- Node Proxy Server Throughput
- CPU Utilization (All CPUs)
- Per Processes Group CPU Usage
- Account Processes CPU Usage
- Container Processes CPU Usage
- Object Processes CPU Usage
- Memory Utilization
- Node Interface Bandwidth
- StatsD Statistics
- OpenVPN Traffic
- Top 4 Node Process Groups by RSS
- Object Replicator Operations
- object-updater sweep Timing and Count

- object-replicator.partition.update Req Timing and Count
- Proxy Req Timing and Count
- account-replicator replication Timing and Count

These metrics and graphics are available under the `View all graphs for this cluster` menu.

What to Look For

When analyzing SwiftStack monitoring data, the following are the key metrics to keep an eye on:

Async Pendings

An `async pending` is a file that is created when an object is uploaded and there is contention to update a container listing record. If this backs up or the container servers gets busy, it will throw an error and then the object server will write to disk a record that says "hey, this container needs to be updated to increment this number of bytes by one object." So that thing on disk that needs to be written later is called an `async pending`. Those are normal in a Swift cluster. It's not a crime to have `async pendings` on your disk, what you need to watch for is if they're accumulating. That's a problem.

What is important to track here is the amount of `async pendings` over time. If you're seeing your rate of generation go way up in comparison to the rate at which they're serviced, that would be something to look into. Perhaps there is too much contention and the account/container records need to be distributed across more or higher-performing media.

CPU Utilization

Load isn't an interesting metric, but one basic machine stat which is important is CPU utilization. Proxy servers in particular are prone to getting CPU-bound and bottlenecking your throughput. This would surface if you under-provisioned your proxy server or a heavy workload comes its way. Another way it could surface is with a large number of request per second, but relatively low volumes of data transfer (for example, lots of HEADs, or PUTs for small objects, lots of GETs for small objects). If you have a workload like that then you'll get a pretty good request per second and your proxy server would be CPU-bound, so watching CPU utilization with proxy servers is particularly important.

The same goes for the back in storage nodes, but it's generally less of an issue because they'll generally get I/O-bound before they get CPU-bound. The possible exception might be an SSD-backed account/container server where your I/O capacity and latencies are so good that your CPU has a chance of becoming bottlenecked.

I/O Utilization

Another metric that's useful is I/O utilization. Those can be tracked per-drive, but rolling them up into a node and cluster view can be really handy. When you have per-drive stats you'll be able to see any hotspots that may show up. This may happen if you have requests that are piling up on a particular account or container. In this case, you will see a huge number of concurrent PUTs to objects within the same container in the per-disk I/O.

Relocation Activity

Relocation activity is useful to watch. If you see spikes that could indicate that a drive is having trouble.

Timing Statistics

There are timing stats for each request. Each part of the request is broken down very granularly so you can pinpoint where issues arise, if they do. You can see if it was an account, container, or an object. You can see the differences between the proxy handling the request and the account/container/object server handling the request. They also get broken down by the verb (GET / HEAD / PUT), so you can get a lot of information out of what each service is seeing.

This means as a Swift operator, you may not be anywhere near the client, but all these metrics can give you a window into the latency that they're observing. You can see whether they're getting a lot of 404s or if all of a sudden some 500s will start popping up. So you can detect problems within the Swift cluster as clients see them.

You really want to catch any problem *before* your clients experience it. All of these internal metrics enable operators to gauge how clients experience the Swift cluster.

Conclusion

In this chapter we covered how to best manage capacity in your Swift cluster; how to deal with the inevitability of drive failures; and how to use the rich and readily available metrics to best monitor your cluster and prevent any problems for your clients or your data. Some key points to remember: add data to new capacity gradually to minimize potential disruption; drive failures trigger replication, while node failures do not; and use StatsD metrics, integrated into SwiftStack to monitor your cluster.

In the following chapters we'll move to integrating (Chapter 8), testing and benchmarking (Chapter 9), and tuning (Chapter 10).

CHAPTER EIGHT

Integrating SwiftStack

As you install and configure your SwiftStack cluster you'll likely need to integrate it with authentication, monitoring, and other systems and services in and outside your datacenter. While requirements may differ from one deployment to another, many common integrations are provided as "add-ons" in the SwiftStack SDS, which do not require significant custom integration work. Other integrations are provided through third-party tools and components, such as CIFS and NFS gateways that support the Swift API.

This chapter provides a high level overview of the most common areas of Swift Stack integration and reviews some of the most common options within each area. Specifically, we will review:

- Authentication
- Billing and chargeback
- Nagios and Ganglia
- CIFS and NFS gateways
- Content Distribution Networks (CDNs)

Note that since each of these areas is highly dependent on your particular use case, workload, and other requirements, this chapter will only summarize each of these integration areas.

Authentication

Swift has a flexible framework for plugging into a variety of different authentication services. Authentication services are deployed as middleware in the proxy tier of your Swift cluster, which makes it possible to integrate with not just one authentication system, but several simultaneously. When selecting which authentication services make the most sense for you, it is important to consider the specific use case you are designing your SwiftStack cluster for. For instance, if your cluster will be used to store and serve data to a great many individual users, a highly scalable system with sophisticated management tools, such as LDAP or Active Directory, might be the right choice. If you expect a moderate number of clients that are continually re-authenticating, a high performing authentication system such as SwiftStack's default authentication system may be most suitable. If your SwiftStack cluster needs to integrate with many other OpenStack subsystems such as Nova and Glance, the Keystone authentication system may be the best route to go. If you are integrating Swift with your CloudStack environment, CSAuth is probably the right option.

SwiftStack clusters can be configured with additional authentication integrations by using the SwiftStack Controller. Here is an overview of the options that are available:

SwiftStack Auth

SwiftStack auth, the default authentication system in SwiftStack, provides a simple and highly scalable authentication mechanism designed to support a variety of different use cases. While similar in structure, the SwiftStack authentication system does not have many of the drawbacks of Tempauth, which stores passwords in clear text and requires a re-start of proxy servers when new users and accounts are added.

The SwiftStack auth system is designed to be fast and simple. A flat-file is deployed on each node with hashed passwords and does not require a proxy restart when users are added or removed. New users can be added via the SwiftStack Controller web-interface. There is also a RESTful API to programmatically add/remove users, which makes it suitable to integrate with other parts of your system. It is also great for application development where there are a fixed number of accounts on the clusters.

Keystone

Keystone is the OpenStack project that provides identity services for OpenStack components. Keystone is very effective when you want to integrate with other OpenStack components. This authentication integration can be used to integrate with other OpenStack services such as storing operating system images and snapshots.

Active Directory

Active Directory (AD) is designed as a special-purpose database to manage large numbers of network originating read and search operations. Data is stored in the Active Directory so that it can be seamlessly replicated; it is built on a hierarchical model; and it is very extensible. Many Microsoft products and end user organizations store user contact data, printer queue information, and specific computer or network configuration data in Active Directory.

Microsoft Active Directory relies heavily on DNS. Most users let the AD manage and provide DNS services for all Windows computers. This facilitates automatic registration of Windows computers that have recently started and/or joined the domain.

SwiftStack supports AD for authentication, which requires a Windows 2008 R2 Active Directory or later implementation. The AD auth module in SwiftStack is an optional add-on, which can be enabled for your cluster. When enabled in the Controller, you simply add your AD domain controller and other information to set up your AD integration.

Figure 8.1

For additional information on the SwiftStack AD add-on, see the SwiftStack Active Directory guide. Contact a SwiftStack representative to request a copy of the guide (*contact@swiftstack.com*).

LDAP

Soon SwiftStack will support LDAP for authentication. Contact a SwiftStack representative for details (*contact@switstack.com*).

SWAuth

SWAuth is an authentication middleware component for Swift that uses Swift itself as a backing store to store account data.

SWAuth is available at: *https://github.com/gholt/swauth.*

SwiftStack allows you to configure and deploy SWAuth authentication middleware through the Controller.

cs_auth

cs_auth is an authentication middleware component developed by CloudOps, which allows Swift to authenticate against CloudStack users.

cs_auth is available at: *https://github.com/cloudops/cs_auth.*

Billing and Chargeback

For many organizations, tracking and billing based on actual usage is a key requirement for a SwiftStack deployment. Service providers need to track and bill their end-customers and internal IT organizations may need to have a chargeback mechanism to bill internal departments for their use. While SwiftStack currently does not provide out-of-the-box integrations with billing systems, SwiftStack will provide a utilization API, that can be queried for utilization data to be used for chargeback purposes.

This utilization API will be queryable by account and a date range which will return a collection of hourly usage data. This data will allow for chargeback calculations including 95-percentile billing. The hourly usage data will include:

- The total bytes used for all the objects in the account.
- The count of all containers.
- The count of all objects.
- The amount of data transfer in.
- The amount of data transfer out.

To query the utilization API an operator would make a GET call to retrieve the utilization data for a particular cluster, account, or user.

Nagios and Ganglia

While extensive monitoring and reporting is provided through the SwiftStack Controller, you might want to integrate with upstream monitoring and alerting systems, such as Nagios and Ganglia. Integration with Nagios and Ganglia can be done in two ways:

- A plugin can be installed on each SwiftStack node, which reports node-level data to a Nagios or Ganglia system.
- The SwiftStack Controller can report cluster and node level data to a Nagios and Ganglia system.

For instance, for Nagios, SwiftStack provides plugin scripts that can be installed on each individual SwiftStack node, including:

- Nagios checker script for unmounted SwiftStack devices.
- Nagios checker script for drive capacity utilization.
- Nagios checker script for background Swift daemons.
- Nagios checker script for the most recent Swift back-end daemon sweep time.

For more information on integrating with Nagios, Ganglia, or other monitoring and alerting systems, contact *support@swiftstack.com.*

CIFS and NFS Gateways

Many applications, especially legacy applications, require a more traditional file interface to the storage system, such as NFS. To bridge this gap, a CIFS or NFS gateway can be used, which provides a more traditional interface to applications and users, but integrates with Swift's native RESTful API for storing and retrieving data. There are currently several providers of gateways, which support Swift's native API, including:

- Maldivica Storage Connector for OpenStack Swift
- TwinStrata CloudArray
- Panzura Global Cloud Storage System
- Riverbed Whitewater Cloud Storage Gateway
- CTERA Portal
- SMEStorage Cloud File Server

When using a storage gateway with SwiftStack (or any other object storage system), it is important to think through the use case properly as there is an inherent level of impedance mismatch between a POSIX-compliant storage interface and an object storage interface since the interface semantics are fundamentally different. If the data is de-duped or compressed by the storage gateway, you can only retrieve the data through the same gateway. This means that any other application needing to access the same data cannot access it directly via the API as it has been transformed before it was stored. This may be ok when the primary use case is to store backups but problematic if other applications need to access the data.

Some gateways, such as the Maldivica Storage Connector for OpenStack Swift, do not have that issue as they write whole files to the Swift cluster. It is therefore important to investigate the underlying mechanics of each gateway and understand how it translates to your specific use case before deciding if a gateway is right for you.

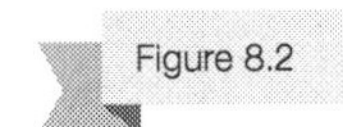
Figure 8.2 ***Configuring the Maldivica Storage Gateway with SwiftStack***

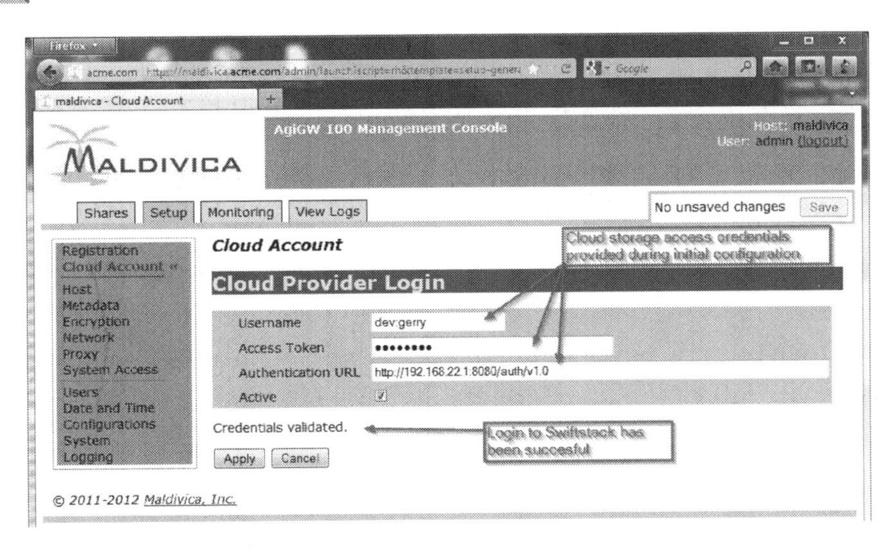

Content Distribution Networks

In Swift, there is native support in the Swift API when Swift is used as an "origin" and integrated with a Content Distribution Network (CDN) provider. For instance, a container in Swift can be CDN enabled and be provided with a CDN URL from the CDN provider your Swift cluster has been integrated with.

When integrating your Swift cluster with a CDN provider, there are several custom integration variables that need to be considered, such as how CDN utilization is tracked and billed. As a starting point, a WSGI middleware component - the Swift Origin Server - provides a starting point for a CDN integration.

The Swift Origin Server is available at: *https://github.com/dpgoetz/sos.*

Conclusion

After this conceptual, high level overview of integrations for SwiftStack you're hopefully ready to do the additional research that you need to make informed decisions for your use cases. The next chapter covers testing and benchmarking.

CHAPTER NINE

Testing and Benchmarking

Before deploying a storage cluster into production, it is prudent to test it to ensure that it operates and performs as expected. The most common categories of testing are:

- Functional testing with the Swift API
- Operations testing
- Failure scenario testing
- Benchmarking testing

This chapter highlights some of the most typical test cases in each category and provides an overview of common benchmarking tools that can be used to test Swift, such as `ssbench` and `swift-bench`. Each environment and workload is unique, though, so while we provide general guidance on testing in this chapter, an individual test plan should be developed for a particular deployment.

Operational Testing

Operational testing allows you to understand and scope the operational effort of adding and removing capacity to a Swift cluster. Some of the operations tests below overlap with the failure testing described later in this chapter.

Below are common operational tests that should be conducted to understand the behavior of the cluster when drives, storage nodes, and proxy nodes are added and removed. When conducting these tests, review the monitoring data to help you determine how to best make capacity changes.

Test: Adding Disks

Adding disks is generally done to add capacity to a cluster. Addition of disks can be done from the SwiftStack Controller and is done by physically inserting a new disk into the server, formatting the disk, and adding it `Immediately` or `Gradually` to the cluster. When adding disks `Immediately` a lot of replication will start in the cluster. When adding disks `Gradually`, the replication processes will take less resources from the cluster and will thus have less impact on operations and users.

Test: Removing Disks

Removing disks is typically only done for two reasons: 1) to replace a disk that is about to fail or 2) to replace a smaller disk with a larger capacity disk. As with adding disks, removing disks can be done `Immediately` or `Gradually` from the SwiftStack Controller. The same caveats apply to removing `Immediately` and `Gradually` as apply to adding disks.

Test: Adding Storage Nodes

Adding a storage node is, again, done mainly to add capacity to the cluster. Adding a node follows the exact same procedure as when first building the cluster. Nodes can be added `Immediately` or `Gradually`. If a large amount of capacity is added at once, as calculated as a percent of your total capacity, it is recommended that you add that capacity `Gradually`.

Test: Removing Storage Nodes

It is relatively uncommon to remove storage nodes. Nodes are typically only removed for two reasons: repair or end-of-life. If a repair might take longer than a few hours – for instance if some parts are hard to find – it might be best to remove the node, assuming there is enough capacity in the cluster. For end-of-life (EoL) nodes, if there is enough space and power in the racks, it might be beneficial to first add the node that will replace the EoL node.

Test: Adding a Proxy Node

Addition of a proxy node is typically done because of an increase in workload.

Adding a proxy node is a quick operation, as no disks have to be formatted and added to the cluster.

Test: Removing a Proxy Node
Conversely, removal of proxy nodes is done because of a decrease in the workload or due to a failure. Again, because there are no disks in a proxy node, removing a proxy node is a quick and easy operation.

Failure Testing

In all clusters, hardware failures are (eventually) inevitable. Hardware failures in a Swift cluster can come in several forms. The most common is a drive failure. Nodes can also become unavailable to the cluster. Should one of these two failures occur, Swift will respond as follows:

- **Drive failure:** Swift assumes the drive might be dead and that it may not be possible to retrieve data from the drive. Thus, Swift will start replicating data to other drives in the system.

- **Node failure:** Swift assumes that the node has become temporarily unavailable due to a power or networking failure, but that data durability is not affected. Hence, Swift will wait for the node to come back. If a node is deleted from the cluster, replication will start to take place in the same manner as when a drive fails.

It is important to understand how Swift operates differently under these different failure scenarios. At SwiftStack we suggests that you simulate common failure scenarios as realistically as possible. Specifically, we recommended that you perform the following failure scenarios to evaluate how *your* Swift cluster responds:

- Failure of a single disk
- Failure of multiple disks
- Failure of a storage node
- Failure of a proxy node
- Data resiliency test

Below are some failure test cases and step-by-step instructions on how to simulate those test failures in your SwiftStack cluster.

Test: Failure of a Single Disk

- Un-mount the disk from the SwiftStack node using Swift Drive Tool commands on the command line
- Watch for a `Device Missing` alert on the SwiftStack Controller
- Mount the disk again using Swift Drive Tool commands
- Watch for a `Device Reappeared` alert in the SwiftStack Controller

Test: Failure of Multiple Disks

- Unmount disk from the SwiftStack node using Swift Drive Tool commands on the command line
- Watch for a `Device Missing` alert on the SwiftStack Controller
- Mount the disk again using Swift Drive Tool commands
- Watch for a `Device Reappeared` alert on the SwiftStack Controller

Test: Failure of a Storage Node

- Disconnect networking or shut down the node from the command line
- Watch for a `Node Missing` alert on the SwiftStack Controller
- Reconnect networking or start up the node again
- Watch for a `Node Reappeared` alert on the SwiftStack Controller

Test: Failure of a Proxy Node

- Disconnect networking or shut down the node from the command line
- Watch for a `Node Missing` alert on the SwiftStack Controller
- Watch the load balancer to look for errors connecting to the proxy
- Reconnect networking or start up the node again
- Watch for a `Node Reappeared` alert on the SwiftStack Controller
- Watch the load balancer to see that the node is reachable again

Test: Data Corruption

- Corrupt data by writing over random parts of a file
- Watch cluster quarantine data and replicate corrected object

Benchmarking

Benchmarking helps you determine if the cluster is sized, configured, and tuned for the desired workload, and if the hardware is capable of handling the expected workload. The goal is to test performance before putting the cluster in production so you can be sure that your cluster will hold up as expected.

There are several Swift benchmarking tools available. The two most used and easily available are:

- `ssbench`
- `swift-bench`

The oldest one is `swift-bench`, which comes bundled with every Swift installation. A newer and more comprehensive test suite is `ssbench` which provides more detailed output. `swift-bench` is good for basic benchmarking and testing, but if you want to do more interesting benchmarking that better matches what you might see in real-world usage of a Swift cluster, `ssbench` is most likely your best choice.

There are also other benchmarking tools that can be used, including COSBench, which is a cloud storage benchmarking tool released by Intel - and commercial benchmarking tools such as Loadrunner. In this chapter, we will review how to use two different benchmarking tools for Swift - `ssbench` and `swift-bench`.

Preparing Your Cluster for Benchmarking

Before you start the benchmarking process you should ensure that your cluster is healthy. Some of the items you may want to check are:

- Networking – check all:
  - cables,
  - NICs,
  - switch settings, and
  - network speeds using iperf and test performance between client to proxy and from proxy to storage nodes.
- To get predictable and repeatable results, it's recommended to remove all data from disks in the cluster before starting benchmarking.
- Before running the benchmark tool make sure that no disks are unmounted.
- Verify that all Swift processes are working properly.

Statistics Tools

Benchmarking in itself provides great information and insight into what your Swift cluster is capable of. However, combined with other tools, like the ones listed below, you can get even more information and learn more about how your Swift cluster behaves and operates.

- iperf - Measures raw network throughput between two NICs.
- httperf - A tool for measuring web server performance.
- htop - An interactive process viewer for Linux.
- iostat - Reports CPU statistics and input/output statistics for devices, partitions and network file systems.
- vmstat - Reports information about processes, memory, paging, block IO, traps, and CPU activity.
- ifstat - Reports network interfaces bandwidth, similar to vmstat/iostat for other system counters.

Measuring Basic Performance

One common performance test is to measure the performance of one single proxy node.

To test a proxy node you can:

- Run `ssbench` from a single or multiple benchmark servers and run them against one proxy node.
- Run `ssbench` with small objects, such as 1 byte or 1 kilobyte objects to find the upper limit by increasing the load on the proxy node until its CPU is running at 100% consistently.
- Simulate many users by increasing concurrency in `ssbench` from just a few (concurrent) users to several thousand users.

Bottlenecks

What you want to look for in your tests is how the different components of your nodes are holding up. The most interesting things to look for typically are:

- High CPU utilization
- Network bandwidth that is at the limit of the interfaces
- High memory usage on storage nodes
- Peak disk I/O

Benchmarking with ssbench

Installing ssbench

Install `ssbench` on your benchmarking machine. The latest version and installation instructions are always available at *https://github.com/swiftstack/ssbench*.

A Basic ssbench Run

`ssbench` comes with a few simple sample scenario files. After you have installed `ssbench`, you can find the sample scenario files in:

/usr/local/share/ssbench/scenarios/

If you want to run one of the sample scenarios, you could run the following:

```
ssbench-master run-scenario \
-A http://<cluster-api-ip>/auth/v1.0 -U <username> -K <key> \
-f /usr/local/share/ssbench/scenarios/very_small.scenario \
-u 4 --workers 2
```

The example above would run the very_small.scenario file with a concurrency (-u), or "users," of four (4) and two workers (--workers). The workers are roughly equivalent to the number of CPUs in your benchmarking machine. You can experiment by raising and lowering the number of workers to see what happens to the number of requests per second that your cluster can handle.

Taking ssbench Further

You can and should of course make `ssbench` do a lot more than the simple `ssbench` run we just tried. Creating your own scenario files is easy. It's just a matter of editing a `json` file. The only thing you want to be mindful of is that you pay attention to commas and other little details in the scenario files, because one comma too much or too little, may cause the scenario file to not run properly.

- Generate an `ssbench` test profile, a so-called "scenario" file, or use the sample files provided by SwiftStack.
- Run `ssbench` in multi-server mode, using more than one benchmarking node at a time.
- The default directory in which `ssbench` will store its result statistics (.stat) file is under */tmp/ssbench-results*. From this directory you can re-generate your reports at a later time.

- Check the resource utilization on the SwiftStack controller at *https://platform.swiftstack.com.*
- For individual and real-time monitoring of each SwiftStack node, you can use tools such as htop, iftop, iostat and vmstat, as mentioned earlier.

SwiftStack can provide you with a zip file including a variety of scenario templates. To get the template files, please contact SwiftStack Support at *support@swiftstack.com.*

Defining Use Cases

There are many use cases for Swift and Swift will perform differently based on the workload and use case. Therefore you should use different scenario files in order to best simulate the load the cluster will be under given your specific use case(s). Some common examples of use cases are:

- Backups
- Applications running directly against Swift
- Photos
- Mail archiving
- Data sharing

In the `ssbench` scenario files you can "nest" multiple file sizes, or file size ranges, which is useful when trying to simulate a certain use case. For example, if you want to test the expected performance of your Swift cluster when mainly used for backups, then you could come up with a set of file size ranges that would be representative of the backup sizes you would expect. Nesting the different ranges in a scenario file would give you clues as to how the cluster would perform during such a load pattern.

How ssbench Works

For each run `ssbench` goes through a series of steps, as follows:

- Distributes jobs to `ssbench-workers` to perform the benchmarking run.
- Uses the authentication process to retrieve a token and a storage URL. (If you already know the token and the storage URL, you can specify them directly by using the -S and -T command line options.)
- Generates containers for use during the benchmark. (Default is 100 containers.)

- Uploads initial objects. (Depends on the number set by initial_files in the scenario file.)
- Starts the run and collects data on each response.
- Cleans up populated objects in the cluster. (Using the -k option will keep objects in the instead of deleting them.)
- Aggregates responses and calculates results.
- Outputs a report in the shell using STDOUT. A copy of the statistics is also saved in */tmp/ssbench-results* so that you can later regenerate the STDOUT file.

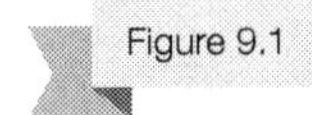
Figure 9.1 ***Sample `ssbench` Report***

```
100M
Worker count:  24   Concurrency: 100  Ran 2013-03-07 19:32:13 UTC to 2013-03-07 19:33:09 UTC (55s)

% Ops    C   R   U   D       Size Range       Size Name
100%   % 100   0   0   0       105 MB           100M
---------------------------------------------------------------------
        100   0   0   0      CRUD weighted average

TOTAL
       Count:   500  Average requests per second:   9.0
                            min       max      avg      std_dev  95%-ile                   Worst latency TX ID
       First-byte latency:  N/A   -   N/A      N/A    (  N/A  )   N/A   (all obj sizes)
       Last-byte  latency:  3.558 -  19.947    8.739  (  3.474)  14.632 (all obj sizes)  tx76d29eb79207482bo448b9045c189f3d
       First-byte latency:  N/A   -   N/A      N/A    (  N/A  )   N/A   (     100M objs)
       Last-byte  latency:  3.558 -  19.947    8.739  (  3.474)  14.632 (     100M objs)  tx76d29eb79207482bo448b9045c189f3d

CREATE
       Count:   500  Average requests per second:   9.0
                            min       max      avg      std_dev  95%-ile                   Worst latency TX ID
       First-byte latency:  N/A   -   N/A      N/A    (  N/A  )   N/A   (all obj sizes)
       Last-byte  latency:  3.558 -  19.947    8.739  (  3.474)  14.632 (all obj sizes)  tx76d29eb79207482bo448b9045c189f3d
       First-byte latency:  N/A   -   N/A      N/A    (  N/A  )   N/A   (     100M objs)
       Last-byte  latency:  3.558 -  19.947    8.739  (  3.474)  14.632 (     100M objs)  tx76d29eb79207482bo448b9045c189f3d
```

Running ssbench

Defining the Scenario File

For defining a scenario file, you can create a file named anything you want. SwiftStack recommends naming the scenario file with a human readable description according to the purpose, size, concurrency, etc.

Upper and Lower Size of Objects

In the real world most storage systems are not used to store files or objects of the exact same size, like 1KB. Subsequently, a benchmarking tool should allow you to randomly specify file sizes or file size ranges. `ssbench` allows you to assign an object size range to perform the benchmarking run. There are two parameters for upper and lower size respectively:

```
"size_min": 4096,
"size_max": 65536
```

Defining Multiple Object Profiles by Name

Real world workloads are also likely to involve multiple object types, usually of different sizes. Therefore, `ssbench` also lets you define multiple object size definitions. Sizes can be anything, but common objects are things like blog posts, photos, backups, VM images, etc. The size of these kinds of objects will obviously would vary. You can simulate different object sizes, and within those a size range, in a benchmarking run by defining nested object name profiles (size category), like in the example below.

```
"sizes": [{
   "name": "tiny",
   "size_min": 4096,
   "size_max": 65536
 }, {
   "name": "small",
   "size_min": 100000,
   "size_max": 200000
 }],
```

Distributing Operation Type Based on CRUD Profile

For each operation of the benchmark run, a size category is first chosen based on the relative counts for each size category in the initial_files dictionary. This probability for each size category appears under the "% Ops" column in the report. Then an operation type is chosen based on that size category's CRUD profile (which can be individually specified or may be inherited from the "top level" CRUD profile).

If each size category has its own CRUD profile, then the overall CRUD profile of the benchmark run will be a weighted average of the values in the "% Ops" column and the CRUD profile of each size category. This weighted average CRUD profile is included in the report on the "CRUD weighted average" line. [3, 4, 2, 2] would mean 27% CREATE, 36% READ, 18% UPDATE, and 18% DELETE.

```
"initial_files": {
   "tiny": 100,
   "small": 10
 },
 "operation_count": 500,
 "crud_profile": [3, 4, 2, 2],
 "user_count": 7
```

Number of Operations and Number of Concurrency

The operations count in a run is determined by the operator. There's no upper or lower limit. To start, you can do a few basic runs with a relatively low `operation_count` in order to get an estimate and a sense of how long a benchmark run would take. Once you have a base case, which gets you a better idea, you can start designing your benchmark plan.

TIP:

- To collect resource utilization, it is recommended to run benchmarks that run for at least 15 minutes. That way it will be easier to view charts on the SwiftStack Controller.

As for concurrency, `ssbench` provides a parameter named `user_count`, which will set the number of concurrent users. By increasing the concurrency you can find the upper limit of concurrent requests for your swift cluster. The bottleneck will be the CPU, network bandwidth, or disk I/O. Higher concurrency may cause:

- Longer CPU queues
- Network bandwidth saturation
- More TCP connections
- More open files in the OS
- Higher latency of each request
- Request timing out

TIP:

- To find a requests per second baseline, you should increase the concurrency (`user_count`) gradually until you start seeing the requests/second trending down.
- To measure maximum concurrent requests, you don't need to run long benchmarks.

As you are adjusting concurrency levels, here are a few items that you can look at to see if you are hitting a ceiling:

1. If you have a specific latency target in mind that your cluster must meet, you can adjust the concurrency and check the latency column in the `ssbench` report to verify the effects of concurrency on latency and adjust concurrency accordingly.

2. If you want to check that all requests were successful during a benchmarking run, you can search the Swift logs (*/var/log/swift/all.log* on SwiftStack nodes) for the word "ERROR." Also, if you have fewer objects in the "TOTAL," as reported in the ssbench report, than what you had specified in your scenario file or on the command line, then you did have some failed operations.
3. If you don't want objects to be handed off to a handoff location, you can check the object-replicator log to find out the maximum concurrency used that successfully completed without handoffs.

The ssbench-worker

The `ssbench-worker`(s) are responsible for performing operations against the Swift cluster and reporting the results to the `ssbench-master`, which in turn will aggregate and generate the final report. The performance of a worker is key for a benchmark run. In general, an `ssbench-worker` will occupy one CPU thread. Given that, it is therefore reasonable to limit the number of `ssbench-workers` to the total number of CPU cores in the benchmarking server.

Before we measure the performance of the Swift cluster, we should find out the maximum load of the benchmark machine itself. You can do that by adding the `--noop` switch as an `ssbench-master` command line option. The scenario will be "run" but the `ssbench-worker` processes will not actually talk to the Swift cluster. Doing this will let you determine the maximum requests per second your benchmarking node is capable of. This number should be higher than what your cluster can produce.

Ways to Start ssbench-worker

There are two ways to start an `ssbench` run. One is from a single server and the second is to use multiple servers, one being the master and additional servers acting as clients.

1. Adding an option `--workers %number_int%` in `ssbench-master` run-scenario command. This is an easy way to call up `ssbench-workers` for a single benchmarking run. This option would be used on a run from a single benchmark machine.

```
ssbench-master run-scenario -f very_small.scenario -u 4 -c 80
-o 500 --workers 2
```

2. Start one or more `ssbench-worker` processes on each server (each `ssbench-worker` process defaults to a maximum gevent-based concurrency of 256, but the -c option can override that default). Use the `--zmq-host` command-line parameter to specify the host on which you will run `ssbench-master`.

```
bench01$ ssbench-worker -c 100 --zmq-host
bench01 1 &
bench01$ ssbench-worker -c 1000 --zmq-host
bench01 2 &
bench02$ ssbench-worker -c 1000 --zmq-host
bench01 3 &
bench02$ ssbench-worker -c 1000 --zmq-host
bench01 4 &
```

Benchmarking with swift-bench

The built-in tool that comes with Swift - `swift-bench` - is pretty good for pushing a lot of load against a cluster. It is a basic distributed benchmarking tool. It allows you to specify a particular workload. You can set the amount of the concurrency per client, the size of the objects that you can upload, the run, and you can provide a range of object sizes to be uploaded from which it will pick a random size for each object. You can specify how many objects to use during the run that will be put into the cluster, and you can specify how many times each object that is put into the cluster will be fetched back out.

Preparation

Make sure that your network and the CPU of the machines that are running the benchmark are not limiting your results; otherwise, you could be testing something other than just what the cluster can do. So, while you are running the benchmarks, you need to make sure that the systems that you are running the benchmarking from are not being limited by the hardware of the benchmark machine itself. If there's a bottleneck, you want it to be in the Swift cluster, not in your benchmarking setup.

How swift-bench Works

For every benchmark run `swift-bench` goes through the following process:

1. It begins by creating containers to put data into.
2. It puts objects into the cluster.
3. It gets objects from the cluster.
4. It then deletes the objects that were put in.
5. It continually generates a report.
6. At the end `swift-bench` deletes the containers it created in step 1.

Overview of Settings

The following settings and associated switches are the main `swift-bench` options:

- Amount of concurrency per client (-c)
- Number of containers to use (configuration file)
- Size of object (-s)
- Random object sizes in a range (-l with -s)
- How many objects to use during the run (-n)
- How many times to GET them after a PUT (-g)

Number of Containers

By default, `swift-bench` only uses a few containers, which may be a limiting factor for your benchmarking run, as this will impact your PUTs and your DELETEs.

When you PUT an object, the object server writes all three replicas to disk. When that happens, the object servers will try to update the container servers so the container servers can maintain an accurate count of both objects and the sum of all of their sizes. Therefore, an object PUT also includes a container update as part of the request. If you are only using a few containers, then there is a possibility that the container server may become the limiting factor.

Another important thing to keep in mind about `swift-bench` is that only a subset of its functionality is exposed via the command line switches and that some functionality is only accessible by settings in the configuration file.

Note that the number of containers to be used can be specified in the configuration file. It's a good idea to distribute the load against hundreds of containers. That way your PUT upload isn't constrained by your container servers which would be fighting over a small set of containers.

Testing High Concurrency (-c, -b)

`swift-bench` will put as much load against the cluster as it can. In other words, it will go as fast as it can given the limitations of the concurrency that you specify. This is because `swift-bench` uses Eventlet under the hood just like Swift does, therefore `swift-bench` does an extremely good job of managing a large number of concurrent network connections even though it's a single process. This means that a single `swift-bench` instance can generate quite a bit of highly concurrent load.

If you're trying to simulate the load of hundreds and hundreds or possibly thousands and thousands of clients, then cranking up the concurrency is how you would do that. For example:

```
$ swift-bench -c 100
```

To test the concurrency even further, SwiftStack added the ability to run `swift-bench` in client-server scenario. This allows a benchmark run to use multiple servers. Each client will listen for benchmarking commands from the 'driver' and report back results. This allows you to use one `swift-bench` invocation to see the results of multiple benchmarking clients. There's a separate command line tool called `swift-bench-client` which is the client and swift-bench has a -b option. `swift-bench` will carve up the load, send it out, and aggregate the results that come back. So there are some limitations to that client-server approach. There's no coordination between the clients, so one client could finish with its portion of the PUTs and start in on its GETs while other clients are still PUTting. So when you carve up a workload that way, it's not directly comparable to a single `swift-bench` client running the same specified load.

Generally, you will want to do that on separate machines so you can get 20, 30, or 40-1 gigabit clients hitting your 10 gigabit cluster. Then, crank up that concurrency as needed.

Again, make sure that something like networking on your client side – where you're trying to generate the load – is not unrealistically limiting the load that goes into the cluster. So if you want to saturate 10G or multiple 10G links into your proxy servers, you're going to need a lot of clients and you're going to need them on potentially a lot of different network cards. If you have two or three 10G boxes to run `swift-bench` on then that's fine. In that case, you can start up a couple of clients on each machine to make sure that you're utilizing more than one CPU core.

Testing Latency

When you benchmark with a concurrency of something small, for example, two:

```
$ swift-bench -c 2
```

the rate will be predominated by the latency of each request because it's only doing up to two requests in parallel. So if that's the case then that test run would be particularly sensitive to the request latency. Therefore, if you're trying to target benchmarking request latency you would set your concurrency low.

Object Size (-s)

The -s is the size of each object to upload. This allows you to see how your cluster performs with various object sizes. For example, you could know what it would do with 100-megabyte objects coming in. Obviously, your request per second will go down depending on how much bandwidth you've got available.

A neat thing to test is to set the value to 0 bytes. That way you can stress out your proxy servers to see how many requests they can field.

Number of Objects (-n)

The -n is the number of objects to be put into the cluster. The size of the objects being put in and the count have an impact on how much storage to use in the cluster, so if you're just playing around with this on the SwiftStack VirtualBox appliance (available at: *http://swiftstack.com/training/swift-install/*), you won't want to go too crazy or you will fill up the little toy disk. So, keep that in mind.

The -n is the number of objects, -g is the number of times that GET requests will be made for objects. The value of -g really doesn't need to be particularly related to -n.

Don't Delete Option (-x)

The -x says don't DELETE, so it basically skips the DELETE phase. So it will neither delete the containers nor the objects that `swift-bench` uploads. This is useful if you want to fill up a cluster with data for other testing purposes. (Do note -- there was a bug with -x in previous versions of `swift-bench`, so make sure you're running Swift version 1.7.5 or newer.)

Running swift-bench

Creating a Configuration File

Create the a configuration file with the following contents, updated for your environment and account settings. Do note, that when doing benchmarks, be sure to create enough containers to support the workload you are testing. Unlike AWS S3, Swift likes to use a lot of containers.

```
[bench]
auth = http://swift.example.com/auth/v1.0
user = benchmark-test-user:test-group
key = testing-password
num_containers = 20
```

Sample swift-bench Run

A sample small swift-bench run, with a concurrency of 20, 10-byte objects, upload 100 objects, then GET 100 objects, would look like this:

```
$ swift-bench -x -c 20 -s 10 -n 100 -g 100 /etc/swift/swift-bench.conf
swift-bench 2012-10-10 15:33:21,764 INFO Auth version: 1.0
swift-bench 2012-10-10 15:33:22,816 INFO Auth version: 1.0
swift-bench 2012-10-10 15:33:24,826 INFO 77 PUTS [0 failures], 38.4/s
...
```

Running a Distributed swift-bench

When trying to generate the load required to benchmark a Swift cluster, it's not unrealistic to need a lot of clients on each machine and to use multiple machines to run the benchmarking.

To do so, there is a client called swift-bench-client, which you run with the options swift-bench-client <ip> <port>

On the benchmarking client run:

```
$ swift-bench-client 192.168.100.2 7000
```

It will listen for its share of the benchmarking workload.

Then on the 'master' benchmarking node, run swift_bench with the -b <client ip>:<port> for each swift-bench-client that is listening.

Example:

```
$ swift-bench -b 192.168.1.2:7000 -b
192.168.1.10:7000 -x -c 10 -s 100 -n 100 -g 100
```

Sample swift-bench Config

For reference, the is an example swift-bench configuration file available on github. This configuration file can serve as a starting point for your benchmarking runs.

https://github.com/openstack/swift/blob/master/etc/object-server.conf-sample

```
[bench]
# auth = http://localhost:8080/auth/v1.0
# user = test:tester
# key = testing
# auth_version = 1.0
# log-level = INFO
# timeout = 10

# You can configure PUT, GET, and DELETE concurrency independently or set all
# three with "concurrency"
# put_concurrency = 10
# get_concurrency = 10
# del_concurrency = 10
# concurrency =

# A space-sep list of files whose contents will be read and randomly chosen
# as the body (object contents) for each PUT.
# object_sources =

# If object_sources is not set and lower_object_size != upper_object_size,
# each PUT will randomly select an object size between the two values.  Units
# are bytes.
# lower_object_size = 10
# upper_object_size = 10
# If object_sources is not set and lower_object_size == upper_object_size,
# every object PUT will contain this many bytes.
# object_size = 1

# num_objects = 1000
# num_gets = 10000
# num_containers = 20
```

```
# The base name for created containers.
# container_name = (randomly-chosen uuid4)

# Should swift-bench benchmark DELETEing the created objects and then delete
# all created containers?
# delete = yes

# Without use_proxy, swift-bench will talk directly to the backend Swift
# servers.  Doing that will require "url", "account", and at least one
# "devices" entry.
# use_proxy = yes

# If use_proxy = yes, this will override any returned X-Storage-Url returned
# by authentication (the account name will still be extracted from
# X-Storage-Url though and may NOT be set with the "account" conf var).  If
# use_proxy = no, this setting is required and used as the X-Storage-Url when
# deleting containers and as a source for IP and port for back-end Swift server
# connections.  The IP and port specified in this setting must have local
# storage access to every device specified in "devices".
# url =

# Only used (and required) when use_proxy = no.
# account =

# A space-sep list of devices names; only relevant (and required) when
# use_proxy = no.
# devices = sdb1
```

Conclusion

In this chapter you've learned how to test and benchmark your Swift cluster. These tools can help you determine the limitations of your deployment and correct for these limitations, if need be. The final chapter (Chapter 10) covers tuning your Swift cluster.

CHAPTER TEN

Tuning

Tuning will have a dramatic impact on the performance of a SwiftStack cluster. In the SwiftStack Controller, there are over 80 tuning settings for Swift. With SwiftStack, it's extremely easy to manage and change those tuning settings. Just go to the tuning section of the Controller and adjust the account, container, object and proxy tuning settings.

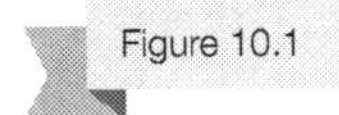

Figure 10.1 ***Tuning settings page in SwiftStack Controller***

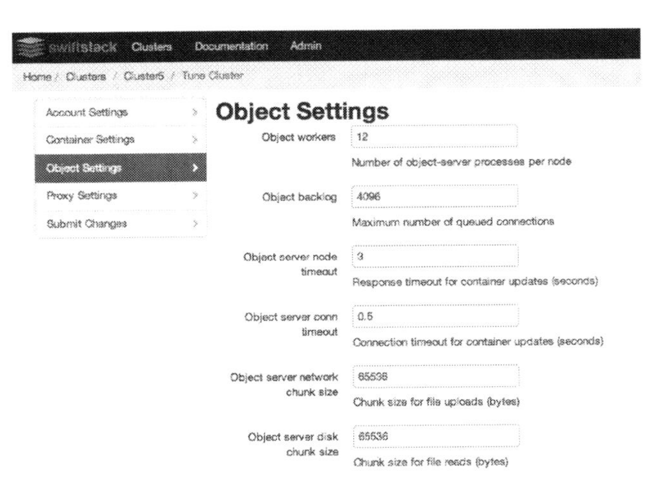

When running benchmarks, you can also visualize the bottlenecks with a comprehensive set of graphs and then make appropriate adjustments on the Swift tuning page. The SwiftStack Controller will then automatically push out the updated configuration settings, and reload the Swift processes, all without any client downtime. This ensures that you are getting the most out of your hardware and that you're are optimizing the performance for your use case.

Here are some of the most common tuning settings in a SwiftStack Cluster:

Worker Settings

Swift Workers
One of the most important tunables that Swift has is the number of workers for each of its primary servers. account_servers, container_servers, object_servers, and proxy_servers all have a setting in their config files called workers.

Proxy Server Workers
One thing to know about Swift is that each worker is accepting sockets off whatever the main binding point is for that server. The proxy server is the easiest to understand because it binds its own port and IP combination and when a new request comes in, it gets accepted by one of the workers. So each worker has a separate UNIX process, and within a single worker up to 1,024 requests are juggled simultaneously using Eventlet. (Eventlet is a green-thread based library for high concurrency in Python.) So what that means is if you know that 10,000 simultaneous concurrent requests are expected to come in to your cluster in production then you can do the math on how many worker processes are needed. Because each proxy server worker can only juggle 1,024 simultaneous requests then, we know that we need at least 10 workers.

Keep in mind that the proxy server workload tends to be CPU-bound because it's not doing any disk I/O, but rather just shuffling network data. This is because of the way Eventlet works. Each worker can only use up to one CPU core. So if you've got a lot of cores in your proxy server (and that's a good idea by the way), you need a good number of workers to be able to saturate them.

A good starting point would be to have one proxy server process per CPU core.

Account, Container, and Object Workers

The account, container, and object servers are not only juggling network traffic from the proxy, but they're also accessing data on disk. For the account and container servers it's with the SQLite databases and if it's the object server – the actual objects. So for all of those, you need enough workers so that your loadable file system operations – like read and write for instance – don't end up starving the Eventlet event loop.

This is because asynchronous network I/O works great, but asynchronous file I/O on pretty much every platform is terrible. So it's important to remember that a read and write system call on Linux can block.

So for object servers, you might need to be sensitive to the request latency that your clients are observing as you're putting load into the cluster because if you have too few object servers and your disks are starting to get saturated then you'd expect clients to see inconsistent latency. Let's say a client is trying to pull a 3-gigabyte file out. If other people or other concurrent connections are utilizing the disk pretty hard then some reads and writes will get blocked. This is because other connections in the same green thread or the same object server worker that your large file stream is coming from will end up blocking the stream that you're pulling. One way to minimize that is to have a larger number of object workers.

The number you should set varies widely depending on your hardware and your network configuration. We won't give you a lot of particular numbers because what's important and what should drive your decisions is the metrics you observe with testing. A good starting point, however, is to run 1-2 processes per spindle or one per CPU core.

Background Daemons

In addition to the servers, there are other background daemons that run in Swift, specifically auditors, replicators, updaters, and the reaper. When tuning Swift, it is important to know how these work and how they can be configured.

Auditors

Auditors are responsible for ensuring the integrity of the stored data. They constantly check it, catch bit-rot, and flag other ways that the data can kind of go stale. So even with three replicas you don't want to just let them sit there or they'll rot as sector failures are not uncommon.

Replicators

Replicators are the eventual consistency guarantors of Swift and will synchronize missing data within the cluster.

Reapers

The reaper is the account reaper and when an account is sent to be deleted, it's deleted asynchronously. When a user, issues a delete, it's marked as a kind of soft-delete. The account reaper is responsible for coming through and actually removing the objects in the containers within the account and then eventually removing the account record. That's an expensive operation depending on size of the data involved, so it's done asynchronously.

Updaters

The updaters are responsible for bubbling up the object and byte count from objects into containers and from containers into accounts.

Background Daemon Settings

One of the common concerns that Swift operators have when they first start is the amount of resources consumed by the background processes. When folks start up their Swift cluster and put a bunch of data in it we often hear, "Oh my gosh look at all of the disk I/O traffic, there's read I/O all over the place and there's only a little trickle of write I/O! What's going on here? I'm not even running `swift-bench` or any other benchmarking tool!"

What's happening is that the background daemons are doing their job.

However, if that level of background work is too high and you wanted to rein them in or tame your background daemons then there are some settings you should know about.

For the auditors there's an "Auditor Interval" setting that determines what interval they run at. Then for the object auditor, there is an additional files-per-second and a bytes-per-second and a zero-byte-files-per-second. So those settings can be used to rate limit the auditing process which will subsequently rate limit its load on the I/O subsystem or CPU.

For the replicators, there are two primary settings. First is concurrency, which is the number of simultaneous outstanding requests each replicator has. If that's too high then you will see more rsync traffic and you'll see more request traffic as one server is asking the other "hey, what version of this do you have?" Then there's run-pause, which is the period of time that the replicator will sleep in between its looping runs.

Then for the reaper there's interval (which is the frequency of the runs) and concurrency (which is the number of items to do in parallel). There's a trade-off here. With higher concurrency you're able to do more and get higher throughput, but at the same time you get higher load. So if you want to lower the load, you can lower the concurrency. On the other hand, if you lower the load and lower the concurrency, you'll raise the time it takes from start to finish for cleaning up a given workload. So that's the trade off you have to make as an operator.

For the updaters there are three variables that you can adjust: interval (discussed above); concurrency (also discussed above); and slow-down which is another rate limiting variable that defines how long to sleep between every update. This allows for a bit more fine-grained control for slowing down the updaters.

Tuning Settings Outside of SwiftStack

There are also tuning settings outside of SwiftStack that an operator needs to be aware of, which can significantly affect the performance of a cluster. These include:

Max Connections Setting for rsync

The max connections setting for rsync may in some cases be a limiting factor on replication traffic.

Enabling Jumbo Frames

Enabling jumbo frames will allow the cluster to get decent throughput with high bandwidth network connections. Even on a 1-gigabit network you're going to get higher throughput with jumbo frames. All of your networking equipment in the chain also needs to be jumbo frame aware, capable, and enabled. The tools for testing that configuration is outside the scope of this book.

ip_conntrack_max

If you're using iptables on the systems or any modules that involve connection tracking, then you absolutely need to bump up ip_conntrack_max.

Chunk Sizes

In addition to rsyncd max connections and jumbo frames, another setting in Swift is chunk sizes. When the proxy server receives a request, it reads data from the client in chunks. So you want your chunk sizes to be large enough that your system calls into the kernel get a decent amount of data back without incurring an overhead cost for going into and out of the kernel-mode with your system calls. We're not going to give you any hard numbers, but you can tune this and see how the CPU utilization of your proxy servers under a given load can change. If you drop that client chunk size down to, something like 1024 bytes or anything lower than the MTU of your jumbo frame network then you might see an increase in CPU utilization. If your clients are coming out of the Internet then they're getting chunked outside your control and so again there's tuning to be done there.

So, when should you use larger chunk size? What are the trade-offs between smaller vs. larger chunk sizes?

A decent rule of thumb is to start with something sizable and then if that has trouble then drop it down some. For example, if it's pretty large like 64 kilobytes then what that means is you're asking the kernel "hey, give me 64k of data" and maybe the client's trickling them in slower than that. Then that means that a read system call will not be blocking because you're using non-blocking network I/O, but you can have higher latency between asking for that chunk and dealing with the chunk.

In some cases a call could take so long that you think there's a timeout or the client just went quiet on you. Well, no it's just dribbling data in so slowly that the kernel's network buffer hasn't filled up in order to satisfy your read request. So, you don't want to set it too high. On the other hand, if you set it too low then you just have the additional overhead of issuing a system calls going in and out of the kernel for each little chunk of data without allowing the kernel to accumulate and then hand it back to you in one batch. So that's the trade-off you need to negotiate.

And again, your testing with your workload is really going to be what needs to inform how you set chunk sizes for your cluster.

For the proxy server, there's the client chunk size which is the chunk size with which the proxy server tries to read client data from the client. Then there's the object chunk size which is the chunk size used when dealing with the object server. This means that they can be independently tuned. This is useful when you have a different internal storage network and a public access network with respect to the proxy server. Then, the traffic coming to the proxy server is not jumbo framed because it's coming in off the internet and you can bump up the object chunk size because it's on a nice fat LAN connection coming from the proxy server to the storage nodes.

Lastly, there is the disk chunk size for dealing with data to and from disk. Disk chunk size and network chunk size from the object server have the same concerns as the proxy server which is you don't want data to be coming in and out of the kernel more than you have to.

Conclusion

Now you've learned about some key tuning variables for getting the best performance out of your SwiftStack cluster. In general, we've tried to give you a conceptual understanding of what different tuning variables do so that you can experiment and determine what is best for your use case.

AFTERWORD

It's Your Turn

Thanks for spending some time with, *Software Defined Storage with OpenStack Swift*. We hope it's been helpful and informative. Now you've reached the end and it's your turn – in two ways.

First, it's your turn to really start applying and working with Swift, SwiftStack, and anything else that you're integrating with. We hope that this process will be satisfying and fulfilling. There's a great community of Swift operators and developers you can turn to for help. And we're always happy to hear from you (*contact@swiftstack.com*).

Second, it's your turn – if you wish – to share with us your comments, feedback, and suggestions. We're planning to produce a second edition of this book and we're very interested in your sense of what we need to correct or add. Thanks, in advance, for helping us create a resource that will serve you better. You can share comments and feedback by visiting *http://swiftstack.com/book/*.

Thanks and we look forward to hearing from you, working with you, or just seeing you around.